HIP-HOP ARTISTS

TRAVIS SCOTT

LO-FI HIP-HOP CREATOR

BY JILL C. WHEELER

Essential Library

An Imprint of Abdo Publishing
abdobooks.com

ABDOBOOKS.COM

Published by Abdo Publishing, a division of ABDO, PO Box 398166, Minneapolis, Minnesota 55439. Copyright © 2020 by Abdo Consulting Group, Inc. International copyrights reserved in all countries. No part of this book may be reproduced in any form without written permission from the publisher. Essential Library™ is a trademark and logo of Abdo Publishing.

Printed in the United States of America, North Mankato, Minnesota.
102019
012020

THIS BOOK CONTAINS RECYCLED MATERIALS

Cover Photo: Scott Roth/Invision/AP Images
Interior Photos: GSAA/ZDS/WENN/Newscom, 4, 87; Tinseltown/Shutterstock Images, 7, 90; Featureflash Photo Agency/Shutterstock Images, 9; Kathy Hutchins/Shutterstock Images, 12, 82; Chris Pizzello/Invision/AP Images, 14; Shutterstock Images, 16–17, 23, 73; Troy Taormina/USA Today Sports/Newscom, 20; Christian Bertrand/Shutterstock Images, 24–25; Johnny Nunez/WireImage/Getty Images, 26, 28–29; Daniel Boczarski/VEVO/Getty Images Entertainment/Getty Images, 31; Shutterstock Images, 32–33; Jamie Lamor Thompson/Shutterstock Images, 36; Jerritt Clark/Roc Nation/Getty Images Entertainment/Getty Images, 38–39; Rob Latour/Rex Features, 42–43; Justin Ng/Retna/Avalon.red/Newscom, 45; David Goldman/AP Images, 48–49; Robb Cohen/Invision/AP Images, 51; SYSPEO/Sipa/Newscom, 52–53; Jack Fordyce/Shutterstock Images, 55; Kevin Mazur/Coachella/Getty Images Entertainment/Getty Images, 60–61; Sky Cinema/Shutterstock Images, 62–63; Swan Gallet/WWD/Rex Features, 65; Pierre Suu/GC images/Getty Images, 68; MHD/PacificCoastNews/Avalon.red/Newscom, 70–71; JOCE/Bauergriffin/Splash/Newscom, 76; Jessica Kourkounis/Houston Chronicle/AP Images, 78; Ian Maule/Tulsa World/AP Images, 81; Anthony Behar/Sipa USA/AP Images, 88; Gary Miller/Getty Images Entertainment/Getty Images, 94; Abaca Press/Hahn Lionel/Abaca/Sipa USA/Newscom, 97

Editor: Megan Ellis
Series Designer: Laura Graphenteen

LIBRARY OF CONGRESS CONTROL NUMBER: 2019941944
PUBLISHER'S CATALOGING-IN-PUBLICATION DATA

Names: Wheeler, Jill C., author.
Title: Travis Scott: lo-fi hip-hop creator / by Jill C. Wheeler
Other title: lo-fi hip-hop creator
Description: Minneapolis, Minnesota : Abdo Publishing, 2020 | Series: Hip-hop artists | Includes online resources and index.
Identifiers: ISBN 9781532190216 (lib. bdg.) | ISBN 9781532176067 (ebook)
Subjects: LCSH: Scott, Travis (Jacques Webster)--Juvenile literature. | Rap (Music)--Juvenile literature. | Songwriters--Juvenile literature. | Sound recording executives and producers--Juvenile literature. | Singers--Juvenile literature.
Classification: DDC 782.421649--dc23

CONTENTS

CHAPTER ONE
HIP-HOP TRANSFORMED
4

CHAPTER TWO
GROWING UP IN H-TOWN
14

CHAPTER THREE
ALL OR NOTHING
26

CHAPTER FOUR
OWL PHARAOH AND *DAYS BEFORE RODEO*
42

CHAPTER FIVE
RODEO AND *BIRDS IN THE TRAP SING MCKNIGHT*
52

CHAPTER SIX
KYLIE AND STORMI
62

CHAPTER SEVEN
ASTROWORLD
76

CHAPTER EIGHT
THE SKY'S THE LIMIT
88

TIMELINE	98
ESSENTIAL FACTS	100
GLOSSARY	102
ADDITIONAL RESOURCES	104
SOURCE NOTES	106
INDEX	110
ABOUT THE AUTHOR	112

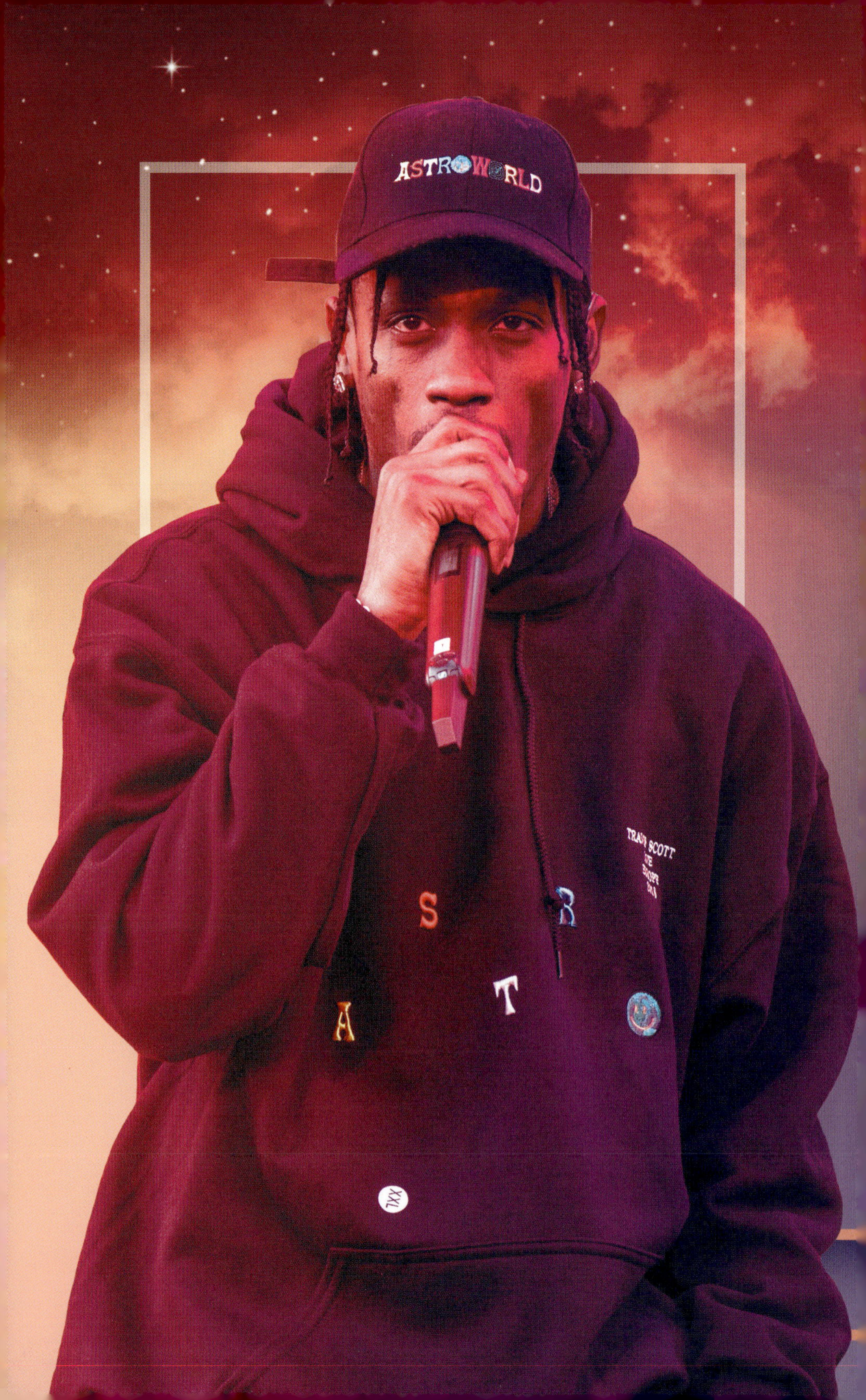
ASTROWORLD

HIP-HOP TRANSFORMED

Chapter ONE

Travis Scott was both excited and nervous. It was the spring of 2012, and he was about to board an airplane to Los Angeles, California, from Texas, where he had recently been going to school. He knew he could afford neither the plane ticket nor a place to stay in Los Angeles. The only thing he knew for certain was that he simply had to go.

It was all about an urge to become somebody by making music. Scott, a native of Houston, Texas, knew from previous experience that Los Angeles was the place to make it happen. As his plane arrived at the gate in Los Angeles, Scott turned on his phone. A deluge of text messages flooded the screen. They were from none other than rapper T.I. and his team. The messages invited Scott to stop by the studio to discuss Scott's work.

Travis Scott got his big break in the music industry in Los Angeles, California.

Kanye West thought Scott was a talented rapper. He signed Scott to his record label in 2012.

After impressing T.I., Scott was later offered a chance to sign as an artist with T.I.'s Grand Hustle Records label. Other doors opened soon after. Scott then signed with Kanye West's G.O.O.D. Music record label as an in-house producer. A producer manages the creation and recording of a song in the studio. He or she may also oversee the song as it is recorded. Scott also signed with the label Epic Records as a hip-hop artist.

For Scott, being signed to a label was more than just a sign of success. It was proof that his instincts had been right all along. Scott's parents had stopped supporting him financially when he left college. They were frustrated after the 20-year-old spent the money they had given him for schoolbooks on trips to Los Angeles and New York City. Instead of books,

KANYE WEST AND G.O.O.D. MUSIC

G.O.O.D. Music is a music label founded in 2004 by rapper Kanye West. The label works to recruit new talent and assist signed artists with music publishing, marketing, and copyright enforcement. West is the founder of the label, though rapper Pusha T was appointed president of G.O.O.D. Music in 2015. G.O.O.D. stands for "Getting Out Our Dreams." G.O.O.D. Music has signed some of the biggest names in the business, including John Legend, Kid Cudi, Common, and Big Sean.

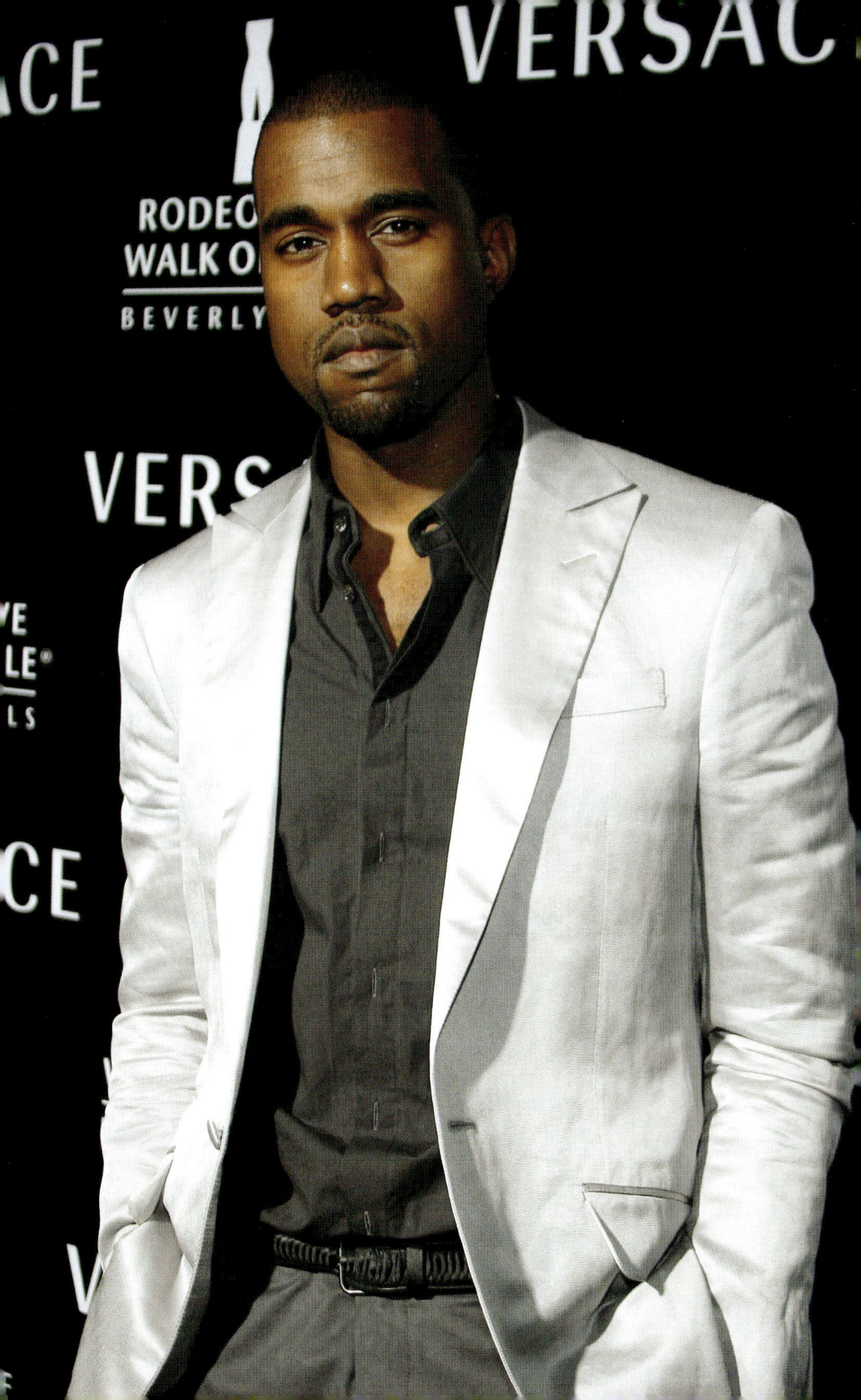
VERSAC
RODEO
WALK OF
BEVERLY
VERS

Scott had invested the money in trips to the coasts and his music production to convince the music industry that he was worth pursuing. Now, all the nights spent on friends' couches or sleeping in cars were about to pay off.

AN ICONIC SOUND

In the years since that fateful flight, Scott has become much more than an up-and-coming young rapper. He has been hailed as a pioneer of a new kind of sound, mixing heavily Auto-Tuned singing and rapping with low, heavy beats. His productions have been called both droning and hypnotic. Scott himself has said he does not like to be boxed in by one musical genre. Yet that has not stopped him from being credited as playing a crucial role in transforming the sound of hip-hop.

After the emergence of hip-hop into the mainstream during the 1990s, many hip-hop artists were slow to

---

T.I. AND GRAND HUSTLE RECORDS

Grand Hustle Records is a record label based in Atlanta, Georgia. Rapper T.I. founded the label in 2003. However, T.I. spent 2009 through 2011 in prison for weapons possession and a parole violation. T.I.'s time in prison weakened the label's reputation, but he returned to the label determined to make up for lost time. Grand Hustle went on to sign artists such as Iggy Azalea and Travis Scott.

Dr. Dre is a famous rapper and producer.

employ technology in the same ways as artists in other genres, such as pop, jazz, rock, and R&B. Music technology had evolved considerably in the 1980s, and hits from the 1990s employed the futuristic sound afforded by new methods. Digital synthesizers and drum machines changed the way music was being made. But hip-hop artists did not embrace these new technologies until the emergence of rapper Dr. Dre in the late 1990s.

A few notable names raised the standards of sound engineering during the 2000s. Yet the experimental creations Scott released in the early 2010s left many

"I always wanted to know how to rap. I was just trying to tell my life story, trying to explain who I am."[1]

– Travis Scott

AUTO-TUNE

Auto-Tune is a technology used to correct pitch. Pitch is the highness or lowness of a sound. The method can correct errors in pitch in real time, by using a pitch detector to exchange the recorded pitch for a desired one. It first was used as an intentional, stylistic choice by artist Cher in her 1998 hit "Believe."[2]

Auto-Tune has become increasingly popular in mainstream music over the past few decades. It often is used to expand music to new and different levels of creativity. In hip-hop, Auto-Tune can turn rappers into singers.

critics confused. They did not know what kind of music he was making. He became known for combining instrumentals that didn't seem to be compatible. His work would transition beats abruptly mid-song. Sometimes he would forgo traditional song formats in the interest of techniques that had not been heard before in mainstream hip-hop.

Scott opened the door for a new wave of younger rappers. He collaborated with a long list of contributing musicians when creating his distinctive new sounds. In the process, he earned himself a reputation in the industry as an artist with a vision.

A REVOLUTIONARY SUCCESS

Scott produced three studio albums before he turned 30. He has spent time atop both the *Billboard* 200 album list and the *Billboard* Hot 100 singles list. In February 2019, he performed at Super Bowl LIII. He also received a Grammy nomination for best rap album for his 2018 album, *Astroworld*. Scott has written and produced music with some of the most well-known individuals in the music industry, including Rihanna, Drake, and Kendrick Lamar, as well as Kanye West and T.I.

> "The word beauty means a lot to me but it all comes down to who you are as a person. It has a lot to do with your heart, how good you are to others."[3]
> – Travis Scott

In addition to catching the eye of his musical peers, Scott's work has been recognized throughout the industry. His first mixtape, *Owl Pharaoh*, was nominated for Best Mixtape at the 2013 Black Entertainment Television (BET) Awards. Yet *Owl Pharaoh* was only the beginning. After releasing *Astroworld*, Scott received even higher praise. Talk show host and comedian Ellen DeGeneres called Scott the "voice of a generation," referencing his popularity with teens and young adults.[4]

"Me and Drake been working to make something so crazy for the kids. It's dope that ['Sicko Mode'] went No. 1. . . . What's more sicko mode than going No. 1?!"[5]
– Travis Scott

> **Drake and Travis Scott have collaborated on several songs.**

Despite his success, Scott never forgot the support he received from his family. After making it big, he decided to repay his parents for the money they gave him for school that he instead used to get a start in music. He bought them a new house in a wealthy suburb of Houston and surprised them with two new luxury cars.

Scott may be young, but he already has achieved a level of success few people will ever reach. His passion for music, his ability to think outside the box, and his unwillingness to give up has made Scott the musician he is today.

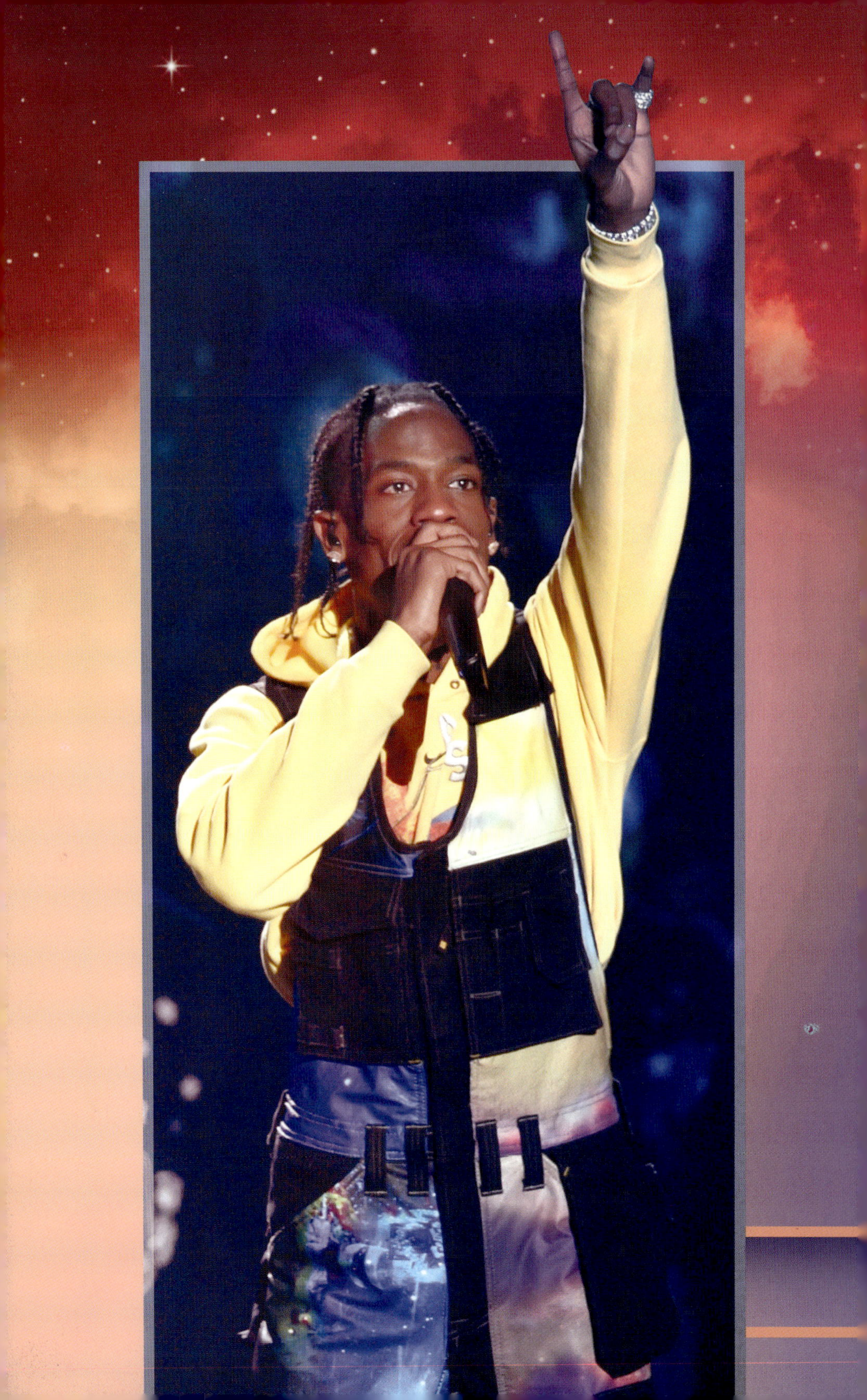

GROWING UP IN H-TOWN

Chapter Two

Travis Scott was born Jacques Bermon Webster II on April 30, 1991, in Houston, Texas. "Travis Scott" is a stage name. Scott chose it because of his admiration for his Uncle Travis. His Uncle Travis was nicknamed Scott and played the bass. Scott also has said that he chose the name in part because of his esteem for rapper Kid Cudi. Kid Cudi's real name is Scott Mescudi. Scott has referred to Kid Cudi and his Uncle Travis as his two superheroes. During the early years of his career, Scott stylized his name as "Travi$ Scott."

Scott's first years were spent at his maternal grandmother's house on the southeast side of Houston. He and his family lived with his grandmother in a neighborhood called South Park. Scott's mother, Wanda Webster, sold cell phones. His father, Jacques Webster, owned his own business.

Jacques Bermon Webster II performs under the stage name Travis Scott.

Houston, Texas, was the fourth-largest city in the United States as of July 2019.

Scott grew up with one sibling, an older brother named Marcus. Marcus has autism. Like many other individuals on the autism spectrum, Marcus has trouble communicating with others. However, he enjoys drawing. He also is a big fan of singer-songwriter Beyoncé.

Scott says he makes sure to buy Marcus a Beyoncé CD every Christmas, even if she has not come out with a new album. Marcus's influence follows Scott wherever he goes on tour. Scott says he knows his brother would be thrilled to meet his favorite artist. Every time Scott brings a fan up on stage, he thinks of his brother.

After many years in South Park, Scott and his family moved to Missouri City, Texas. Missouri City is a middle-class suburb outside of Houston. Even though he spent his later years in the suburbs, Scott said his proximity to his grandmother's lower-income neighborhood had a lasting impact on his life.

LIFE IN THE SUBURBS

While living with his grandmother, Scott attended private school. He then transferred to a public school for high school. He recalls seeing big differences between his own home life and the lives of his private school classmates. Seeing these

KID CUDI

Travis Scott says that he feels inspired and influenced by Kid Cudi. Many other performers feel the same way. Kid Cudi often is regarded as a founding father of alternative hip-hop. He has been one of the most well-known and well-regarded artists of the genre in the past decade. Originally from near Cleveland, Ohio, Cudi rose to fame with the hit single "Day 'N' Nite" in 2008. Cudi made the *Billboard* Top 100 11 times with hits such as "Mr. Rager," "Erase Me," and "Pursuit of Happiness (Nightmare)." He rose to fame at a time when hip-hop was undergoing a transformation. His ability to blend indie rock, electronica, and dubstep with more mainstream hip-hop created an ever-growing fan base.

differences instilled a drive in him to create a better life for himself when he grew up. The obvious wealth of his friends from private school only made him want that kind of life more intensely.

He also realized that reaching that goal might take him to a world far beyond Houston.

Scott received his first drum set as a gift from his father when he was just three years old. For many families, a drum set for a toddler would be odd. For the Websters, it just made sense. Scott was a young member of a family full of musicians. His Uncle Travis played the bass. Scott's maternal grandfather was a jazz composer. Scott's father was a soul musician. Another of Scott's uncles worked on a 1990s R&B album that sold more than one million copies. Despite this heritage, Scott's parents were not always supportive of his musical career aspirations. They worried that the music industry would be too difficult and that Scott would have trouble succeeding.

> "Growing up, my grandmother stayed in the hood so I seen random crazy s***. . . . I saw people looking weird, hungry, and grimey. . . . It gave me my edge—[it made me] who I am right now."[1]
>
> – *Travis Scott*

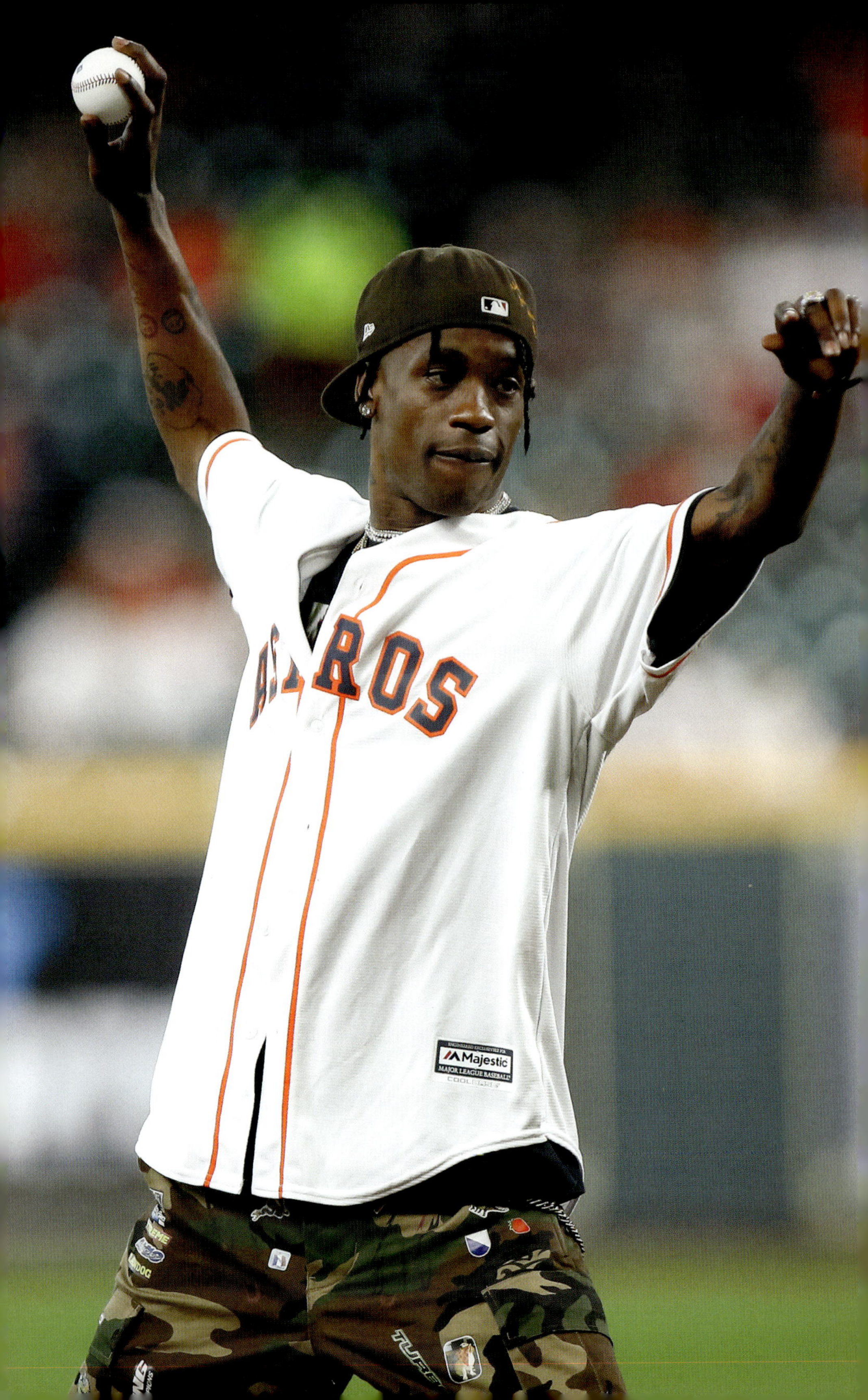
ROS
Majestic
MAJOR LEAGUE BASEBALL

Scott supports his hometown sports teams. In 2019, Scott threw the first pitch at a Houston Astros baseball game.

When Scott was a teenager, his father quit his job in order to pursue music full time. The decision left Scott's mother to support the family. It also left them struggling financially and increased tensions between Scott and his father. The two musicians had frequent arguments. Scott's father would be recording in the den while Scott was making beats in his bedroom. Sometimes, that led to Scott's father shutting off the bedroom's electricity. Scott recalls times when he and his father would argue so much that they would get into fistfights. Today, Scott and his father have a much better relationship. Scott credits his father for passing

JAZZ AND HIP-HOP

Jazz and hip-hop may seem like two completely different musical genres, but they are linked in several ways. Both emerged as a way for African American artists to creatively express themselves to a wide audience that came to include whites. Jazz music emerged in the 1920s. It evolved from ragtime music, which was inspired by slave songs and blues music.

The first recognized hip-hop song was Sugarhill Gang's "Rapper's Delight" in 1980. Freestyle rap can trace its roots back to a specific characteristic of jazz known as scat solos. Scatting is a vocal style that uses improvised nonsense sounds instead of words over a melody. Today, rappers such as Travis Scott, Kendrick Lamar, and Common use jazz to inspire their own music.

along his swag, or his cool way of carrying himself, to Scott.

DEVELOPING A STYLE

Scott started rapping as a teenager. He had learned to play the drums and piano in his childhood, but he knew that to become the artist he wanted to be, he had to start making beats. Rapping over instrumentals, he decided, was just not cutting it. Scott wanted the mood of his music to be darker.

His search for this unique sound became all consuming. He recalls spending so much time studying and creating music at home that he would occasionally skip school to make beats. Despite that, Scott claims he never got in much

HOW DO YOU MAKE A BEAT?

A beat can be a pattern made by a drum or a repetitive pulse that underlies a song. A good beat is essential in genres such as hip-hop, dubstep, and techno. When creating a beat, artists must choose which instruments they'd like to use. Beats often include drums, but almost anything can go into a beat. Clapping hands, rhythmic shouts, and even animal calls can underlie beats. Artists typically create beats in software programs, which let the artist layer different sounds together and adjust other elements of the beats. Once a beat is created, artists can add music and lyrics to bring the song to life.

"I'm big on diversity. My music is very diverse, I don't want it to ever be typecasted."[2]
— *Travis Scott*

People can create beats using music production software.

trouble as a teenager. Instead, he was very involved in musical theater and even acted in several productions, including *Oliver!* and *Kiss Me, Kate*.

At school, Scott was known for his charm and popularity. His friends at Elkins High School in Missouri City recall that he was clearly talented, even at a young age. He almost always had the lead role in whatever show

Scott performs in front of large crowds using experience he gained acting in high school theater productions.

the school was putting on at the time. They remember Scott as being outspoken and having a sense of humor that could make the entire cafeteria burst out laughing.

Scott excelled in school and graduated in 2008, right after turning 17. He applied and was accepted into the University of Texas at San Antonio. Yet formal education had never been his priority. Rather, he viewed this next chapter of his life as an opportunity to dive further into the music industry. He was eager to see how far his creativity and charisma could take him.

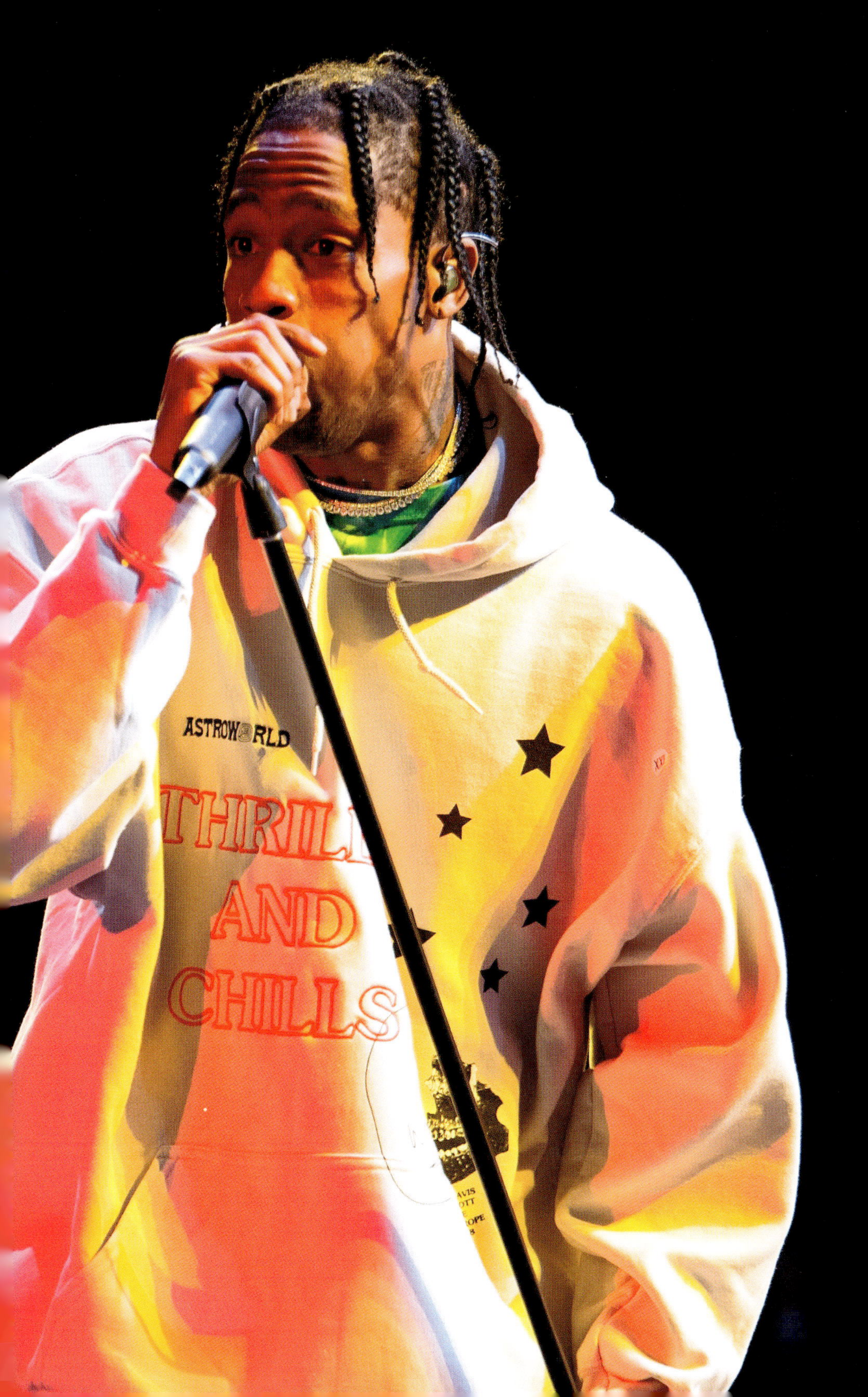
ASTROWORLD
AND
CHILLS

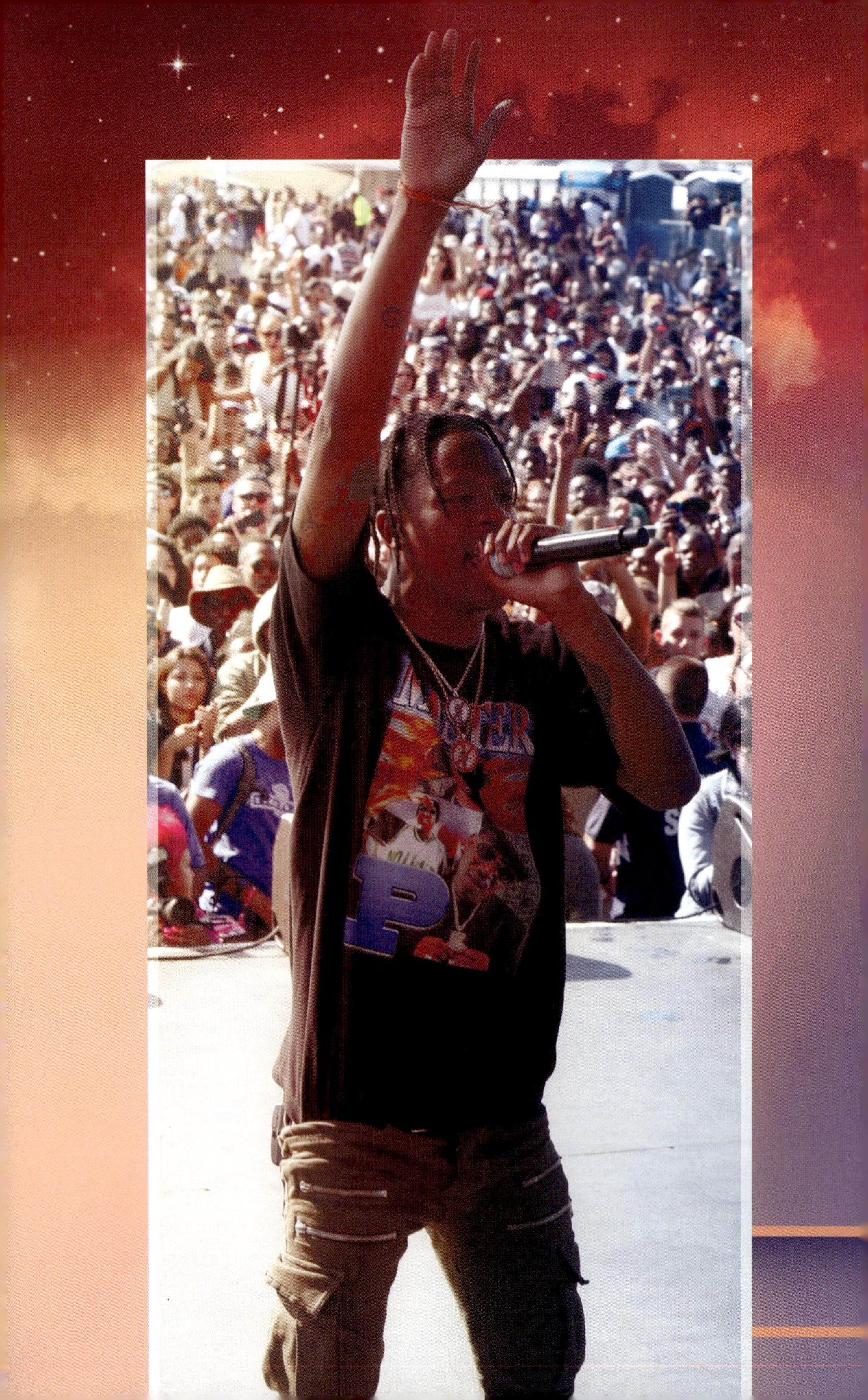

ALL OR NOTHING

Chapter THREE

After high school, Scott began classes at the University of Texas at San Antonio. But by his sophomore year, he was already bored. He recalls feeling as though he was wasting his time in class. He felt he was listening to professors who were teaching him things he didn't need to know. Scott was far more interested in becoming a rapper. For years, all he had wanted was to make music and play sold-out shows. He never had been interested in a desk job.

However, Scott's parents wanted him to graduate from college. His family was full of musicians, but it was also full of college graduates. Like many parents, Jacques and Wanda Webster wanted their son to have a degree. They thought a degree was an important thing to fall back on if his music career didn't work out. They knew that while many young people may want a career in music, only a few actually succeed.

Scott had friends who worked hard in college so they could enjoy successful careers in business or medicine.

While he was in school, Scott dreamed of performing in front of sold-out crowds.

Travis Scott has worked in recording studios with other hip-hop artists such as DJ Khaled.

But many of those same friends were struggling to find jobs after graduation. Scott found that every day spent in classes just made him feel more and more depressed.

Meanwhile, Scott's early efforts as a professional musician had been disappointing. He had worked on a

couple of hip-hop projects in high school and college, but neither of them took off. He had formed a duo called the Graduates with a friend, Chris Holloway. The two released an extended play (EP) in 2009. Scott next formed the Classmates with another friend, Jason Eric. Eric, who today raps as OG Chess, was also a classmate of Scott. Scott and OG Chess had a lot in common, as both were creative aspiring musicians from the suburbs. The Classmates put out a couple of mixtapes with Scott producing. However, the group broke up in 2011. At that time, Scott started to pursue his solo act.

CHASING INSPIRATION

One day, Scott was emailing his friend Mike Waxx when Waxx asked if Scott was in New York City. He wondered if Scott was interested in connecting with other musicians. The question stopped Scott in his tracks. Waxx was the founder and CEO of the music website IllRoots. He also had connections with artists from West's G.O.O.D. Music label. Waxx had even been involved in creating

THE ROLE OF A RECORD PRODUCER

Before he became a star, Travis Scott worked behind the scenes as a record producer. Producers may or may not write songs. Regardless, they are responsible for the final product. Record producer Rick Camp says producers are in charge of everything. "[A producer] calls all the shots on what's played, and when it's played, and how it's played," Camp said.[1]

Producer Donny Baker adds that a music producer should be the person who finds the studio and hires an engineer. The goal is to find people who have worked on similar songs. That way, they know how to help artists make their songs sound the way they need to sound to be competitive.

music videos for some of the artists on the G.O.O.D. label. Scott abruptly decided that he was not going to spend any more time in college. If New York was where the opportunity was, he needed to be there, too.

Scott called his mother the next day. He told her he was running low on funds. He said he needed money for books, as well as a new computer. Wanda sent him the money, and Scott used some of it to fly to New York and meet up with Waxx.

Shortly after arriving in New York, Scott found himself wrapped up in the music scene. He quickly began

West has performed at concerts as part of the G.O.O.D. Music lineup.

Scott decided to pursue a career in music instead of finishing college.

making connections with other rappers and producers. However, Scott spent several months sleeping on couches. He started to feel as though New York could not offer the inspiration that he sought. He began to think that Los Angeles might be a better place to be.

Scott took more of the money his mother had sent him for college and bought a plane ticket to Los Angeles. A friend had agreed to go with him, and the two planned to pool their resources and connections to survive in a new city. Things took a surprising turn after the plane landed in California. Scott's friend chose to part ways with him. Scott found himself out of money and feeling more alone than ever.

CUT OFF

In the meantime, Scott's relationship with his parents had become increasingly challenging. His parents had made a surprise visit to the University of Texas at San Antonio. They expected to find their son there studying and enjoying college life. Instead, they learned that he'd dropped out. What followed was a very angry phone call. Scott tried to explain how necessary his time in New York and Los Angeles had been. His parents did not see things in the same way. After the call, they stopped paying for his cell phone plan.

> "I couldn't be here without my friends. I wouldn't like have a place to lay my head some nights but my friends held me down; that's how much they believed in me."[2]
> – Travis Scott

Despite a rocky start, Scott was starting to make a name for himself in California. He was putting out a lot of music, but he had not made a lot of money doing so. He flew back to Houston, where he planned to live with his parents while working on his music. But his parents had a different idea. They were frustrated and concerned with their son's lies. They also considered his career dream to be an unrealistic one. They refused to let him stay with them or waste any more of their money on his musical career.

Scott did not call it quits. He called up a friend who offered to buy him a ticket back to Los Angeles. That friend connected him with someone who was studying at the University of Southern California and could offer Scott a place to stay. Everything came together for the young musician when Scott received the text messages from T.I. after stepping off the plane. Good things truly began to happen for Scott's music career.

Throughout his cross-country struggles, Scott had been putting music out on the internet. Some hip-hop blogs picked it up and reposted it. T.I. heard a song Scott

> **SOUNDCLOUD**
>
> Scott caught the ear of T.I. via songs he had uploaded to the internet. SoundCloud is an online site where individuals can upload, share, and promote their songs. Prior to SoundCloud, artists were at the mercy of radio stations and live performances to get exposure for their music. Hip-hop in particular has benefited from SoundCloud's broad reach. In addition to Scott, Post Malone, Lil Pump, and Playboi Carti all got their start sharing tracks and gaining fans on SoundCloud.

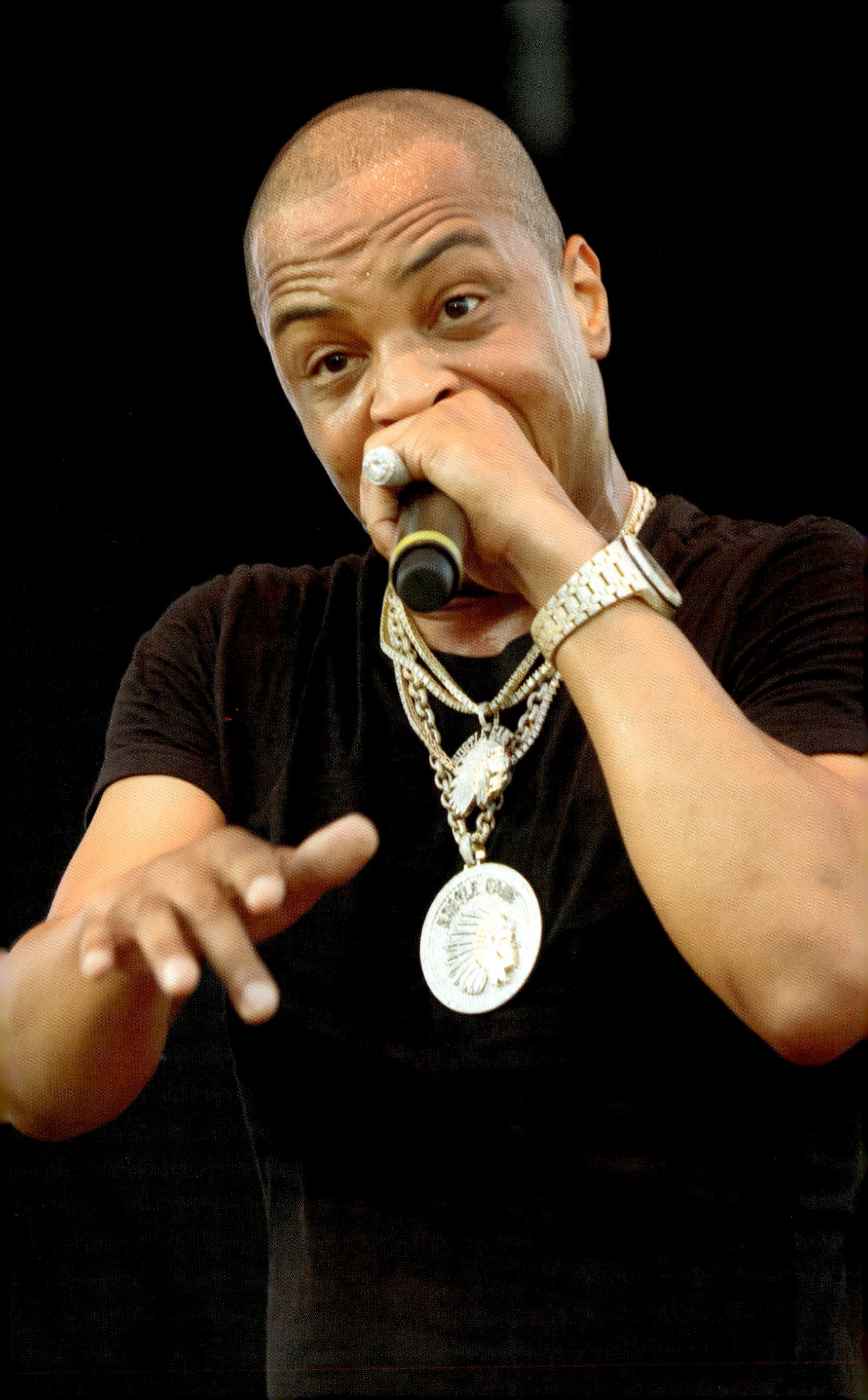

> **T.I. is a rapper and record producer.**

had put out called "Lights (Love Sick)." After consulting with Waxx and other connections, he contacted Scott. He asked if Scott could stop by his studio one afternoon. When Scott came by, T.I. told him that his music was good. T.I. said Scott should keep doing what he was doing if he wanted to become successful.

FIRST MEETING WITH KANYE WEST

Gradually, Scott began making money from his beats. He made enough that he was able to sublease a room in an apartment. At the same time, word was getting around about Scott's talent. Scott found the name of one of Kanye West's sound engineers, Anthony Kilhoffer, in the credits of one of West's albums. Scott emailed him out of the blue. The two connected and hit it off, but Scott didn't know whether anything would come of it. Then, Scott received a call from a friend telling him that Kanye West wanted to meet up with him in New York.

Connecting with West was a dream come true for Scott. He bought a ticket for the next flight to New York. When he met West for the first time, Scott recalls being instantly starstruck. He couldn't believe West had heard of him or his music.

Scott, *right*, performed with other artists affiliated with G.O.O.D. Music, including, *from left to right*, 2 Chainz, Big Sean, and Kanye West.

West asked Scott to play some music for him that first day they met. Scott remembers feeling over the moon when West bobbed his head to a beat. The famous rapper told Scott his music was good. He also offered some feedback here and there.

G.O.O.D. TIMES

The meeting with West turned out to be the first of many. Scott's aspirations were becoming very real. He signed with Epic Records, a major music label owned by Sony Music Entertainment. In addition, Scott became a major collaborator on G.O.O.D. Music's *Cruel Summer*. *Cruel Summer* was a compilation of songs created by the label's various artists. It was scheduled for release in September 2012. *Cruel Summer* had two singles, the most famous one being "Mercy." People who worked on the single included not only Scott but also Pusha T and Big Sean. Common, DJ Khaled, Kid Cudi, John Legend, Jay-Z, 2 Chainz, and, of course, West himself helped create the album.

Scott had never experienced anything quite like working on *Cruel Summer*. He appears only on the song "Sin City," but he was around for the creation of all the tracks. He received production credits for three of the 12 songs. He had not intended to be on "Sin City," but West asked and Scott couldn't disappoint. He was nervous, but he freestyled his verse and nailed it. During his verse, he rapped, "Run from home, after

TACOS WITH KANYE

During their first meeting, Kanye West offered Scott a taco from a fast-food restaurant. He served it on a very expensive plate. Scott opened the taco to discover that it had sour cream on it, which Scott hated. West noticed Scott was avoiding the taco and asked him why. Scott panicked and quickly ate the entire thing. He did not want to make any kind of a negative impression on someone he admired so much. Scott recalls the meeting with West was so exciting that he tried to ignore the lingering taste of sour cream in his mouth while they discussed Scott's music.

tonight, we up out of here / Don't go home, cause they just ran me up out of there."[3]

Cruel Summer gave Scott an experience few up-and-coming artists ever have. He was surrounded by talent. Scott got to know artists he admired, but he also got their advice on succeeding in the industry. At the same time, it was nerve-racking. He was nervous about playing his beats and rapping in front of West. He had idolized West for so long, and now he was in front of him.

EAST COAST SOUND VS. WEST COAST SOUND

New York City and Los Angeles have long been centers of hip-hop. In the 1980s and 1990s, each coast was known for putting out a different sound and backing a different group of rappers.

West Coast hip-hop tended to employ a slower tempo, with an emphasis on interesting melodies and catchy hooks. East Coast hip-hop was known to be darker and more aggressive. It featured a greater emphasis on lyrics than on catchy tunes. The rivalry took a sinister turn in the mid-1990s. A professional relationship between Los Angeles–based rapper Tupac Shakur and New York City's Notorious B.I.G. soured. It resulted in a feud that eventually led to the unsolved murders of both artists.

After his production work on *Cruel Summer*, he joined G.O.O.D. Music's production wing, Very Good Beats. In 2013, he signed on to Grand Hustle Records. By signing with labels and collaborating with other artists, Scott could be sure his music would make it to the masses.

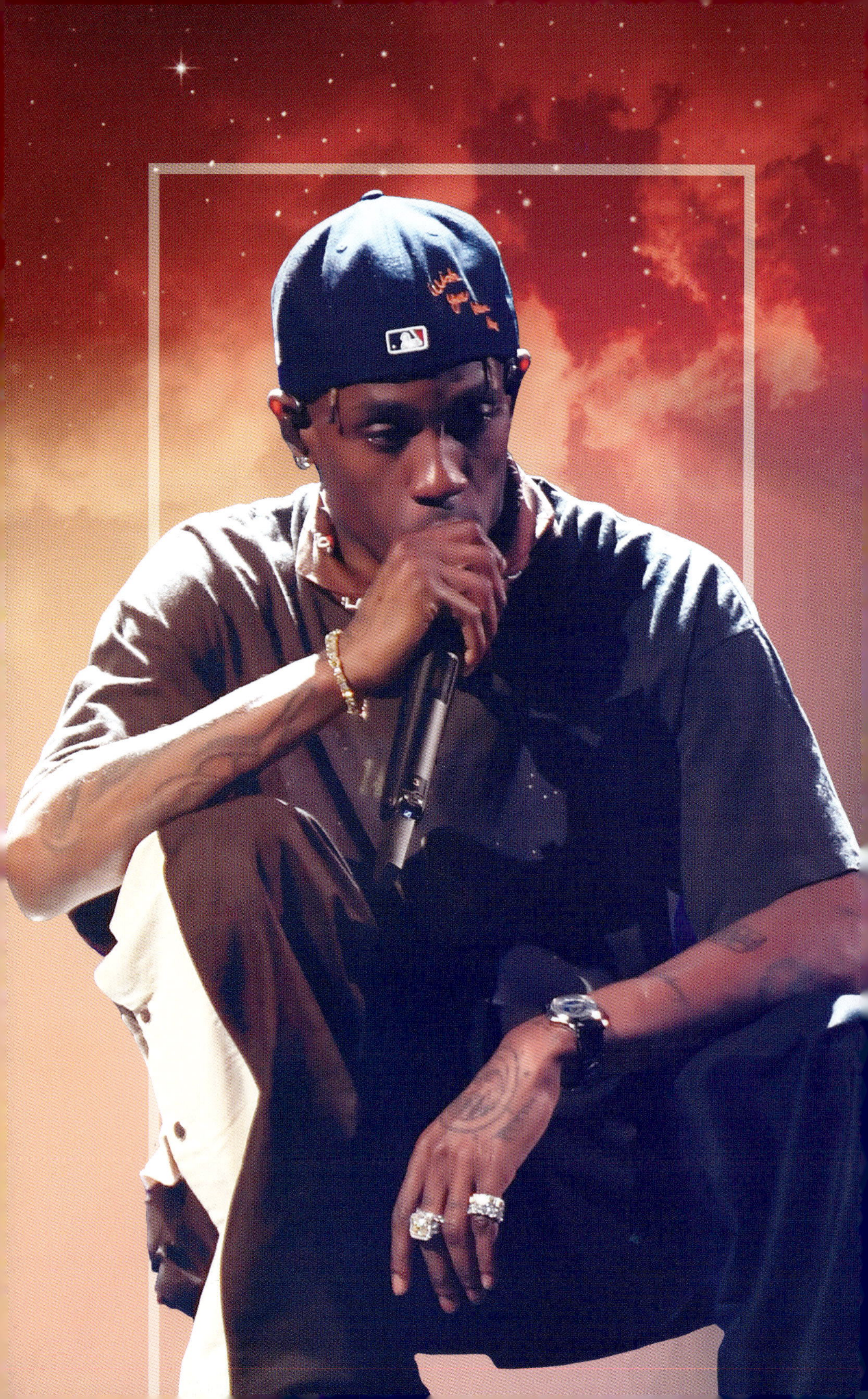

OWL PHARAOH AND *DAYS BEFORE RODEO*

Chapter FOUR

Travis Scott released his first mixtape, *Owl Pharaoh*, on May 21, 2013. He offered it for free on SoundCloud. The mixtape's name reflected his own drive for perfection. Scott's friends called him "Owl" because he was sleeping fewer hours to work on his music.

Owl Pharaoh dropped nearly a year later than Scott intended because he was busy working on other projects and learning more about the industry. The extra time was well worth it, however. *Cruel Summer* plunged Scott into a deeper level of the hip-hop world. Suddenly, he was meeting artists who had inspired him for years. He also toured with G.O.O.D. Music to promote *Cruel Summer* and performed at music festivals around the United States.

Scott travels around the world touring with his music.

Bon Iver front man Justin Vernon worked with Scott on *Owl Pharaoh*. Vernon has also collaborated with other rappers such as Kanye West.

In addition, collaborating on *Cruel Summer* gave Scott a pool of gifted artists who would give him input or offer constructive criticism. Scott had completed a significant portion of *Owl Pharaoh* before signing to Grand Hustle Records and working on *Cruel Summer*. Yet he quickly realized the project needed some serious reworking. He was proud of the work he'd done so far, but he believed his tracks could be even better.

Scott credits T.I., West, and Justin Vernon—the front man of Bon Iver—as having the largest impacts on *Owl Pharaoh*. Those artists, however, were just the tip of the iceberg. The mixtape also features appearances by Wale, Toro y Moi, A$AP Ferg, and Meek Mill, among others. The lead

JUSTIN VERNON

Justin Vernon is a musician from Eau Claire, Wisconsin. He is best known as the front man of the indie folk band Bon Iver. He is not only a singer but also a songwriter, producer, and multi-instrumentalist. Bon Iver has a soft rock sound, yet Vernon is known for much more. He has become a well-known collaborator with many hip-hop artists. His most famed collaboration was with Kanye West on "Monster." Vernon also has worked with Vince Staples, Doomtree's P.O.S., and Lizzo, as well as Scott. His ability to experiment with Auto-Tune has made him a popular feature on today's hip-hop tracks. Kanye West has called Vernon his favorite living artist.

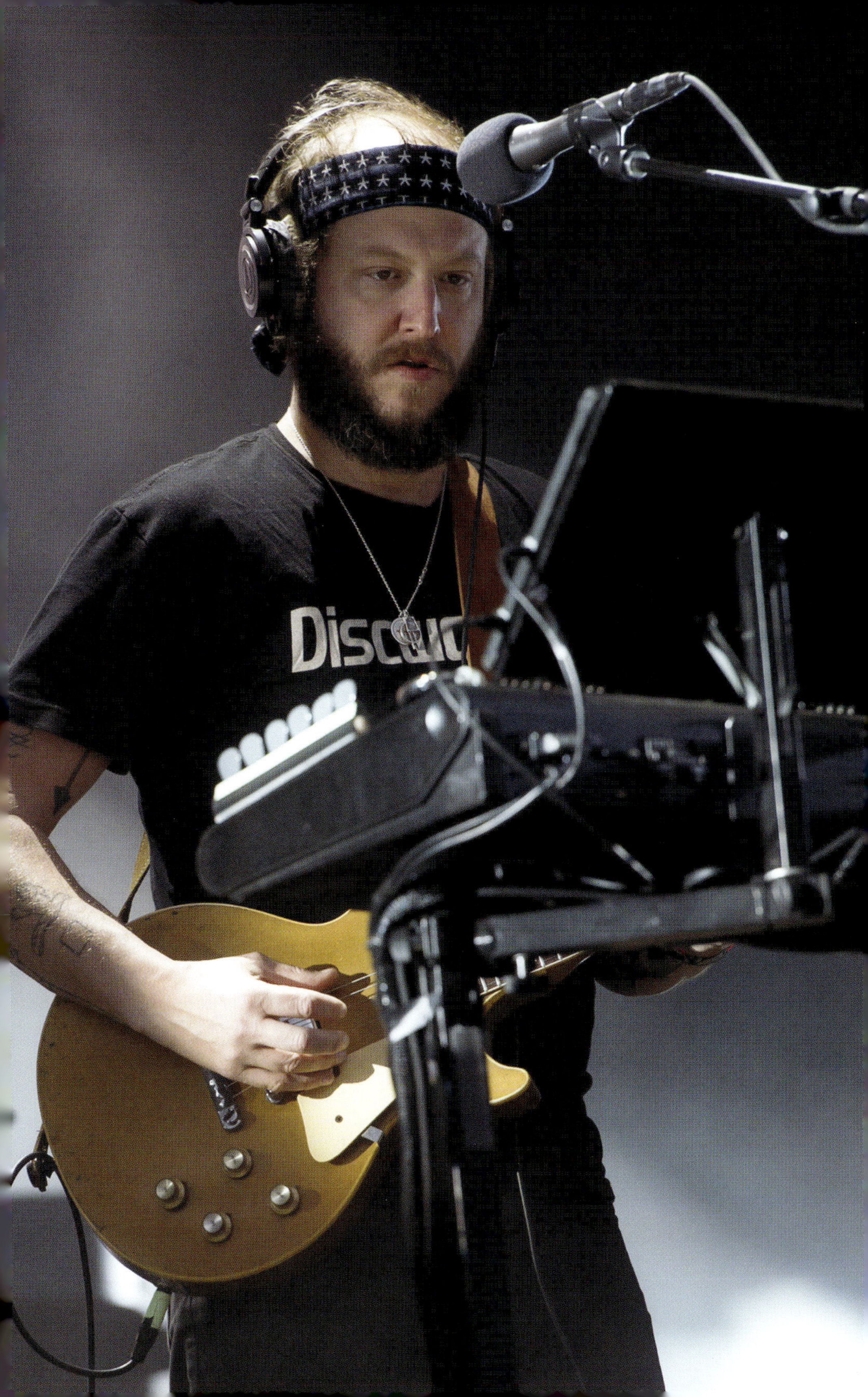

> "I feel like a little thing in my head is telling me I shouldn't drop [*Owl Pharaoh*] yet, that I can probably make this whole story grander. My beats can be way more iller, my raps can be way more iller."[2]
>
> – Travis Scott

single, "Upper Echelon," which quickly became a hit, featured 2 Chainz and T.I.

CRITICAL ACCLAIM

Scott's first mixtape helped get his name out into the mainstream hip-hop world. The contributions by the collaborating artists played an important part. Yet Scott had also woven a work that was uniquely his own. Critics lauded *Owl Pharaoh* as "mesmerizing" and "invigorating."[1]

Scott was named to *XXL Mag*'s Freshman Class of 2013. It was a list of up-and-coming rappers to watch. *Owl Pharaoh* also was included on *SPIN* magazine's 40 best hip-hop albums of 2013.

Achieving some fame did not translate into much of a slowdown for Scott, however. On August 18, 2014, he released *Days before Rodeo*. He emphasized that this new work was to be taken as an album, not a mixtape.

Days before Rodeo was another highly collaborative album. As with *Owl Pharaoh*, Scott released it for free on SoundCloud. Artists such as Migos, Young Thug, Rich Homie Quan, and T.I. joined Scott on several tracks.

The biggest hit was the single "Don't Play." It featured Big Sean and English band the 1975. Once again, Scott's work met with positive reviews. Critics took note of the subtle influence of T.I. and West. They complimented Scott on this latest work. However, one of the greatest impacts *Days before Rodeo* had is the tour that followed.

TEARING IT UP ON TOUR

Set between the releases of *Days before Rodeo* and the forthcoming album *Rodeo* itself, the Rodeo Tour took place between March 1 and April 1, 2015. The tour took Travis Scott and Young Thug to thousands of fans

> "Perhaps Owl Pharaoh's sole drawback is that it still doesn't quite seem to answer the question 'Who exactly is Travi$ Scott?'. Luckily for him, [Owl Pharaoh] is so mesmerizing that everyone should want to find out."[3]
> – *Ralph Bristout*, XXL Mag, *May 2013*

ALBUM VS. MIXTAPE

Travis Scott used social media to tell fans that *Days before Rodeo* was an album, not a mixtape. Both albums and mixtapes can be full-length projects with varying numbers of featured artists. Yet they often have different objectives. Albums follow a more traditional route. They are intended to be sold as individual units and typically offer hit singles. Meanwhile, mixtapes are an excellent way for artists to put their music out for free. They allow new talent to reach larger audiences, stay relevant on social media, and announce new tour dates.

Scott, *left*, and Young Thug performed together at the BET Hip Hop Awards in 2016.

across the continental United States. The three played sold-out shows nearly every night that garnered press attention and even celebrity attendees. At one California show, Kanye West came up on stage. He began singing Scott's lyrics word for word.

The Rodeo Tour quickly garnered a reputation for being absolutely outrageous. One senior editor at online music magazine *Complex* penned a review of the show. It was titled "I Tried Not to Die at Travi$ Scott and Young Thug's Show Last Night."[4] Fans were encouraged to rush the stage and go wild in mosh pits, areas where fans pushed and shoved each other, invigorated by the music. This resulted in an explosion of energy from fans that was set to a steady background of Scott's most popular music.

Scott had created yet another reason to make him unforgettable—a unique performance experience for his fans, who were primarily teenagers and young adults.

One *GQ* writer wrote about seeing Scott perform at a nightclub. Scott was swinging from a chandelier while performing. When part of the fixture cut his hand, Scott simply slapped a bloody handprint on the ceiling and kept right on rapping. Fans lived for the insanity. Even after the Rodeo Tour, Scott's shows remained energetic and occasionally dangerous. Fans frequently were injured. Scott has even been arrested and charged with inciting a riot on two

THE HISTORY OF MOSHING

Moshing, a popular, high-energy concert activity, traces its roots to the hardcore music of the 1980s. Moshing evolved out of general pushing and shoving, fights in the audience, stage diving, and crowd surfing. It's a general term for an intense and aggressive expression of emotion. Moshing spread first into thrash metal, then grunge rock music. In the 1990s, as those genres evolved into the more popular death metal and pop punk, moshing came, too. Shows such as the Warped Tour of the early 2000s were known for their unruly crowds. As the years went on, moshing became increasingly banned at large-scale events, though at Scott's concerts, it was encouraged.

Travis Scott is known for his antics while performing on tour, such as jumping on sound equipment.

separate occasions. One instance was a show at the music festival Lollapalooza in 2015. The other was a 2017 show in Rogers, Arkansas. Scott took the incidents in stride. In response to his arrest after the Rogers show, for which he was charged with inciting a riot, endangering a minor, and disorderly conduct, he sold fans a limited-edition T-shirt. The shirt had his mugshot printed on it above the slogan "Free the Rage."[5]

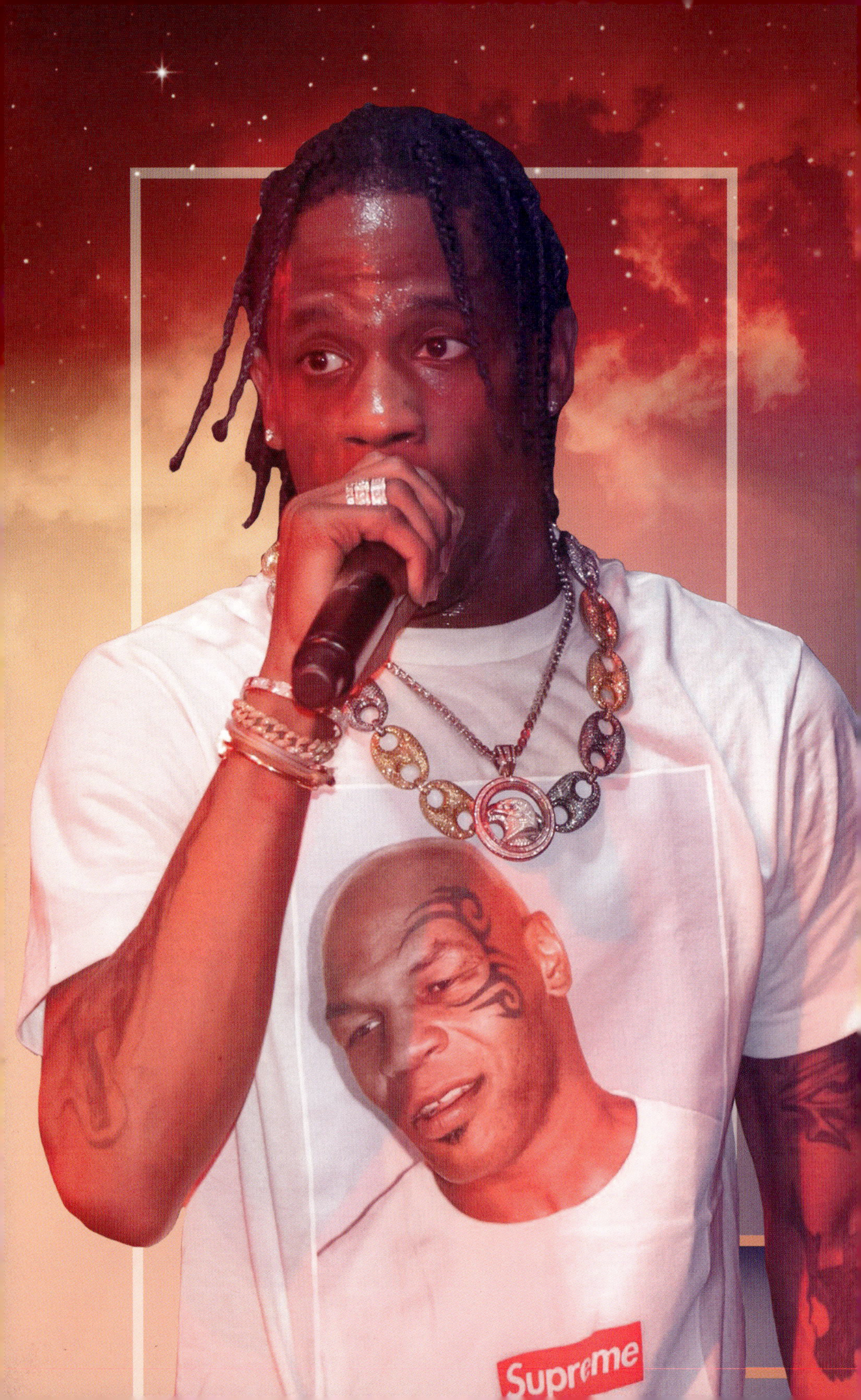
Supreme

RODEO AND BIRDS IN THE TRAP SING MCKNIGHT

Chapter FIVE

Days before Rodeo was intended as a prequel to Scott's Grand Hustle/Epic Records album *Rodeo*, which was released just one year later on September 4, 2015. Scott has reiterated that the albums were not necessarily intended to be similar. *Rodeo* was Scott's highly anticipated first studio album. T.I. said he thought *Rodeo* would be one of the best solo albums of 2015.

Scott said that as with *Days before Rodeo*, he named his solo piece *Rodeo* because he felt as though his life was a rodeo. He said that putting out work and growing as a musician and a star was like riding a bull.

In 2016, Scott performed at venues around the world after releasing *Rodeo* and *Birds in the Trap Sing McKnight*.

> Justin Bieber appears on Scott's song "Maria I'm Drunk."

Rodeo had two hit singles: "3500," featuring rappers 2 Chainz and Future, and "Antidote." "3500" reached gold status. That means it sold or streamed the equivalent of 500,000 units. One download equals one unit, while one hundred streams equals one unit. "Antidote," meanwhile, reached platinum status, selling and streaming more than one million units. These milestones were important in Scott's career. *Rodeo* also included a host of guest appearances by other artists, including Kanye West, Young Thug, The Weeknd, Juicy J, and Justin Bieber.

Rodeo debuted at Number 3 on the *Billboard* 200 and Number 1 on *Billboard*'s Rap Albums after it was released. Eventually, the full album was certified platinum, meaning the album had sold and streamed more than one million units.

MIXED REVIEWS

Reviews for *Rodeo* were mostly positive, but they were not as glowing as T.I. had hoped. One review in hip-hop magazine *XXL Mag* lauded Scott's creative vision. It said the album would bring Scott into mainstream hip-hop in no time. Other reviews were less complimentary. *Rolling Stone* argued that Scott's greatest strength in *Rodeo* was

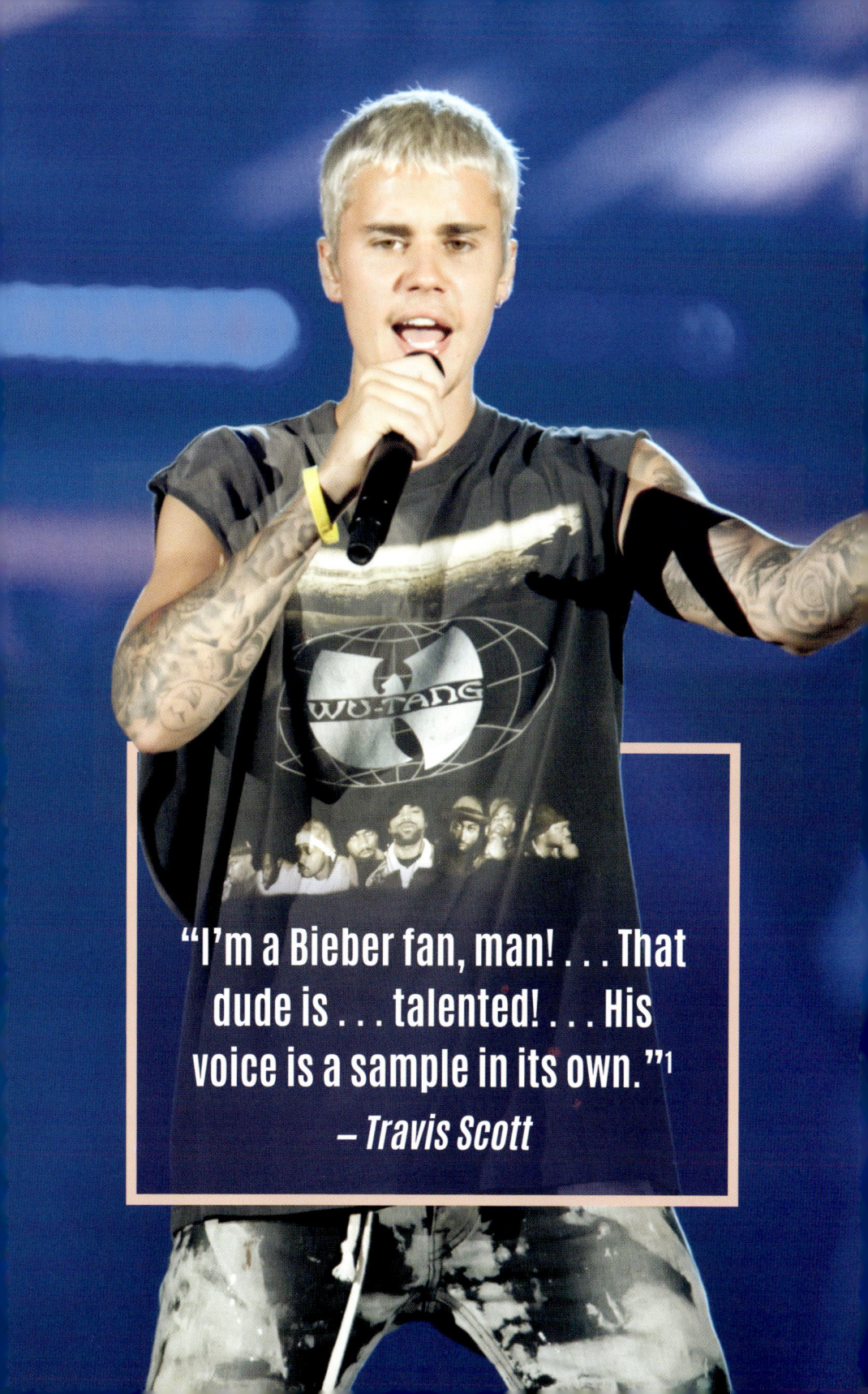

> "I'm a Bieber fan, man! . . . That dude is . . . talented! . . . His voice is a sample in its own."[1]
> – Travis Scott

roping in unexpected talent. The magazine said that some of that talent overshadowed his own vocal abilities.

Rodeo still reached the ears of more than one million fans. They readily welcomed the next installment in the Travis Scott story. Fans also proved ready to purchase more than just music. The cover art for *Rodeo* featured a Travis Scott action figure, which quickly became more than simply art. Upon releasing the album, Scott also released an actual limited-edition Travis Scott action figure for $150. The collectible has since become a popular item among fans. As of 2019, it had retailed for up to $750 on online marketplaces such as eBay and Bonanza.[2]

The same year *Rodeo* was released, Scott was collaborating with several other artists. The credit "featuring Travis Scott" became a popular addition to the titles of hit songs in 2015. Scott assisted with the production of Rihanna's hit single "B**** Better Have My Money." The single went platinum just a few months after its release. Scott also helped write the song "Woo" on Rihanna's album *Anti*. His signature Auto-Tuned voice can be heard singing the "Woooooo" on the chorus.[3] The two musicians were rumored to be dating, but neither ever confirmed any relationship other than a professional one.

Still, the link to Rihanna undoubtedly boosted Scott's name recognition.

> "There's a lot of us out here that are birds, man. We all need to just fly."[4]
>
> – Travis Scott

BIRDS FLYING HIGH

On January 4, 2016, Scott announced via producer Mike Dean's Snapchat that a new album was on the way. *Birds in the Trap Sing McKnight* was released in September 2016. Scott said he named the album for what he and his friends experienced growing up in Missouri City. As he recalls, they felt trapped. It was not because they came from a low-income area, but because they often could not express themselves in the ways they wished.

Birds in the Trap Sing McKnight brought a host of popular artists together who mixed their own voices and

---

SHAPING THE SOUND OF THE NBA

The video for Scott's "Way Back" track on *Birds* features Houston Rockets shooting guard James Harden. A fan of National Basketball Association (NBA) basketball himself, Scott was chosen to executive produce the soundtrack for the NBA 2K19 video game. The game has a long history of featuring the best in rap and hip-hop. As executive producer, Scott selected the full NBA 2K19 game soundtrack. It features selections from Scott's albums, along with Bruno Mars, Cardi B, Migos, and more.

beats into a definitive Scott sound. This included Kid Cudi, Scott's biggest music idol. Scott recalls having cried the first time he met Kid Cudi. Now he was making music with him.

Birds featured Kid Cudi on the track "Through the Late Night." The piece included a portion of Kid Cudi's hit single "Day 'N' Nite." The artist also assisted with the harmonies on "Way Back." In addition, Young Thug and Quavo showed up on the album's first single, "Pick Up the Phone." Andre 3000 from the duo Outkast showed up on "The Ends." The Weeknd, Atlanta-based rapper 21 Savage, and Toronto rapper Nav all contributed to the album too.

However, the biggest hit from *Birds* was "Goosebumps," which featured Kendrick Lamar. Scott had long regarded Lamar as the greatest rapper in the world, and at an MTV Video Music Awards ceremony, Lamar let Scott know he thought his music was inspirational.

"Goosebumps" hit platinum and peaked at Number 28 on the *Billboard* Top 100.

> "I'm just here for good times, man. I want people to have the best time ever. Especially if they're around me. I feel like God put me here to help out with people's soul, man."[5]
>
> – Travis Scott

HITTING HIS STRIDE

Unlike the mixed reception for *Rodeo, Birds in the Trap*

Sing McKnight was met with more positive reviews. *Birds* made it to Number 1 on the *Billboard* 200. One critic at *Clash* applauded *Birds'* continuity. The critic noted that part of what made Scott's music so special was Scott's sensitivity and darkness. *XXL Mag* called it "a roller coaster ride of an experience, with an endless amount of highlights."[6]

Birds solidified what had become Scott's signature sound. It was a crazy mix of the top names in hip-hop, coupled with top-notch production values. *Birds* went on to become one of the 40 best hip-hop albums of the year, according to *Rolling Stone*. *Birds* also extended Scott's proven recipe for success outside the studio. Scott announced the Birds Eye View Tour, which took place from April through June 2017 and traveled across the United States. It also included performances at the Coachella music festival in California.

CACTUS JACK RECORDS

In March 2017, Scott announced he would be creating his own music label. He called it Cactus Jack Records. Some artists create their own label to have complete financial and creative control over their own music. Scott stressed that this was not his motive. He said he wanted to help other up-and-coming artists achieve their own musical dreams. His goal with the label was to give others the opportunities he had. The label has since taken on Sheck Wes and Don Toliver, two rappers who would later collaborate with Scott.

> **During his 2017 Coachella performance, Scott rapped while riding on the back of a giant floating robotic bird.**

As with the Rodeo Tour, the Birds Eye View Tour shows became known for their high-energy antics. Scott went so far as to urge fans to jump off second-floor balconies at some venues. One man who jumped from a third-floor balcony later sued Scott. Scott claimed to be not responsible for the incident. Whenever fans quieted down, Scott reminded them whose concert they were attending: this was a Travis Scott show, and it was meant to be outrageous. Scott was no stranger to surprises while performing, either. Earlier that year, he had been a guest at a Drake show in London, England. As he walked out toward the audience, he abruptly fell through a hole in the middle of the stage. Talking later about the incident, Scott just laughed and said he didn't fall, he flew.

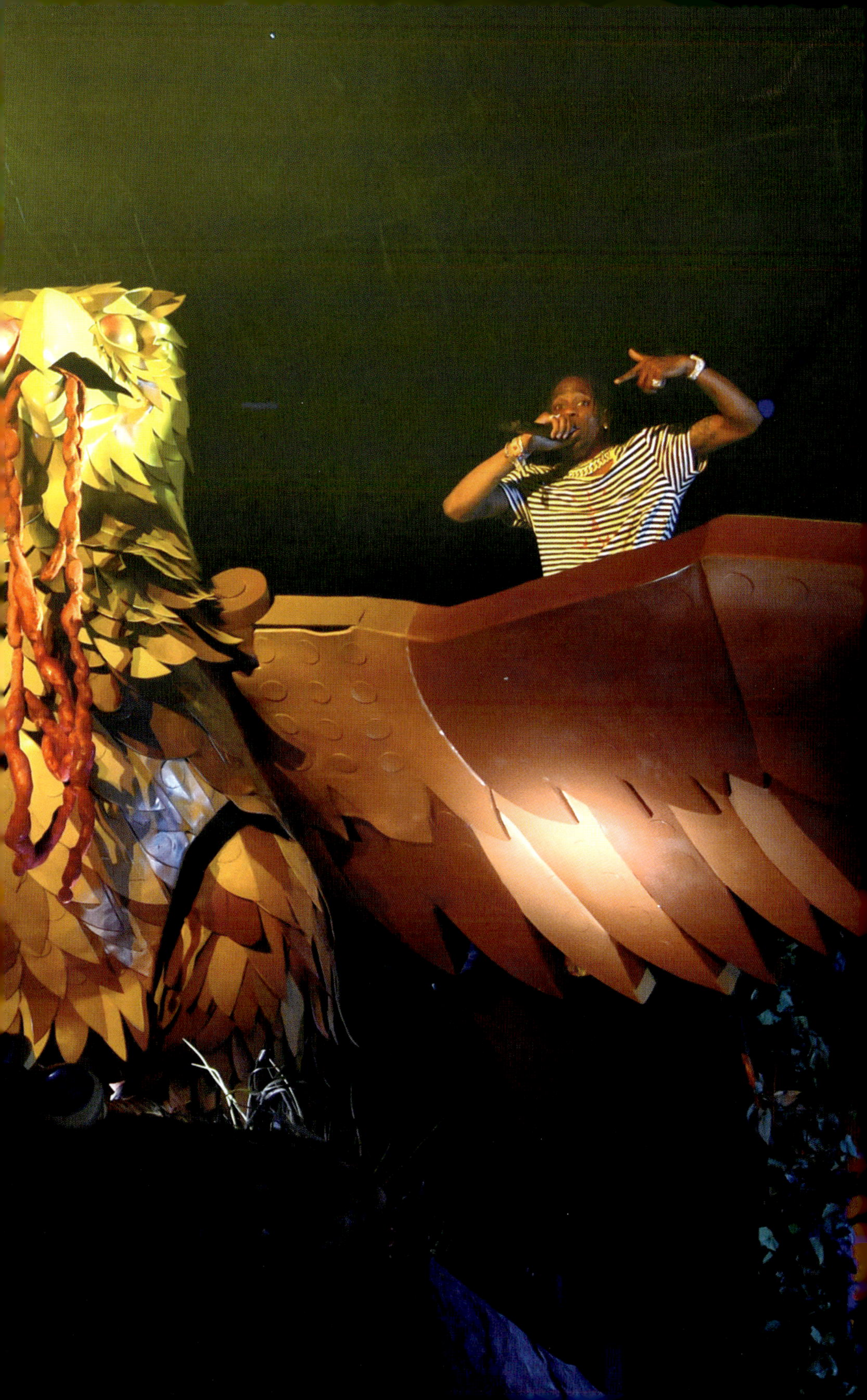

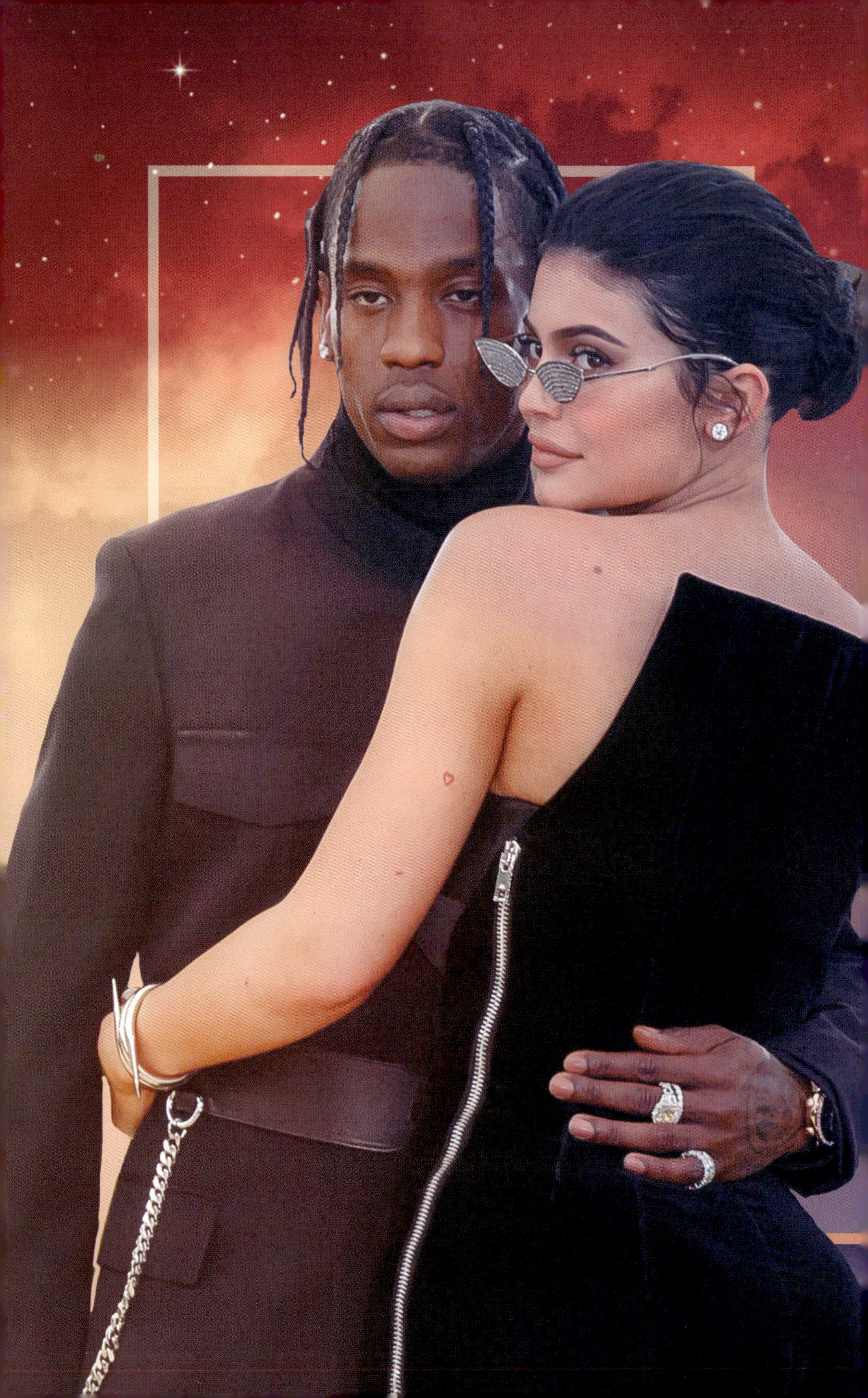

KYLIE AND STORMI

Chapter SIX

Scott's Birds Eye View Tour strengthened his image as a hip-hop powerhouse. It also introduced him to Kylie Jenner. The two met at the Coachella music festival in April 2017. Scott asked Jenner what she thought about seeing him again. In response, Jenner climbed onto his tour bus and followed him for the rest of the tour.

Many fans first learned about Jenner from her family's reality television show *Keeping Up with the Kardashians*. When Jenner was just 18, she began selling her Kylie Cosmetics makeup and skin care line. She also is a social media personality with more than 250 million followers across various platforms.[1] In addition, Jenner was the most watched person on Snapchat for several years. In 2019, Jenner was named the world's youngest self-made billionaire by business magazine *Forbes*.

Scott and Jenner appeared together at the 2018 Met Gala.

By 2017, Scott had experienced life in the public eye. Yet the scrutiny was even more intense for him in the company of Jenner. After being spotted holding hands with Jenner at Coachella, Scott was followed by paparazzi throughout early 2017. The couple sat courtside at basketball games. They explored cities where Scott's tour had taken them. They also attended the 2017 Met Gala, an annual fundraiser held to benefit the Metropolitan Museum's Costume Institute. Top-name designers use celebrities to showcase their most spectacular designs at the event, all in order to garner money for

BUSINESSWOMAN KYLIE JENNER

Kylie Jenner is more than just a social media personality. Jenner began Kylie Cosmetics in 2015, originally selling products exclusively online or via the occasional pop-up shop. In 2018, she signed a deal with beauty retailer Ulta. Ulta placed her lipstick and lip liner kit in the chain's more than 1,000 stores. In just six weeks, Jenner sold more than $50 million worth of her products. Jenner credits her more than 175 million social media followers for her success.[2]

"We ain't run out of a thing to say.... I was like, 'I need her with me to operate. She's that one.'"[3]

— Travis Scott

each year's exhibit. The couple's presence served to unite two passions—fashion and fame—of the young couple. In June 2017, they got tiny matching butterfly tattoos on their ankles and shared photos of them with their Snapchat followers. In August, Scott celebrated Jenner's twentieth birthday with expensive gifts. He surprised her with a diamond necklace and a performance by a string orchestra.

Jenner and Scott often attended events together. In 2018, they went to the Louis Vuitton runway show at Paris Fashion Week.

Scott and Jenner bonded early over a shared love of Tim Burton and Wes Anderson films. They also shared a strong religious faith and a commitment to supporting each other's businesses. Additionally, they prioritized time together. Scott has said he was surprised when he met Jenner and found she was so chill. He had expected her to obsess over her public image and assumed that Jenner would need to be near her security guards at all times. As it turned out, the two were able to relax together and take long walks in whatever city they happened to be in.

WELCOME, STORMI

In September 2017, rumors began to circulate that Jenner was pregnant. However, Jenner, Scott, and the entire Kardashian family kept the secret under wraps. *Billboard* magazine even asked Scott if he'd talked to his own father about becoming a father. Scott evaded the question, saying that fans could keep fishing for details about a pregnancy, but he wouldn't say anything. The pregnancy stayed hush-hush right up until Scott and Jenner's baby daughter was born on February 1, 2018. However, Scott and Jenner did not announce her birth until February 4.

In an interview, Scott told *Rolling Stone* magazine that he had been hoping for a son at first. But when he found out Jenner was having a daughter, he was ecstatic. Scott joined Jenner in the delivery room, even though he was very nervous. He also cut the umbilical cord. The two named their baby girl Stormi Webster, but they disagree on who came up with her name. Jenner released an 11-minute video documenting her pregnancy and the birth to announce Stormi's presence to the world. Scott tweeted that there was a "new rager in town."[4] As for Stormi, she already has proven to be a fan of her father's music. Scott reports that "Stargazing" seems to be Stormi's favorite track.

> ## LIFE IN THE LIMELIGHT
> Kylie Jenner is known for her regular selfie posts on Instagram. Before social media was huge, the socialite was used to being in front of the camera during the filming of her family's reality show. Scott, on the other hand, is no fan of cameras. At a 2018 photo shoot for the magazine *GQ*, Jenner showed up with her own large glamour team, while Scott brought only his manager and spent much of the shoot pacing the room and avoiding cameras. One *GQ* writer equated watching Scott be photographed to watching him undergo "medieval torture."[6] Scott resents anything that makes him waste time, and though he tends to like the end result of hours of shooting, he can't stand the process.

   Scott also gave Jenner 443 roses after the birth. The flowers represented the time Stormi had been born: 4:43 p.m. He then followed up with a gift fitting Jenner's passion for luxury cars: a $1.4 million Ferrari LaFerrari.[5]

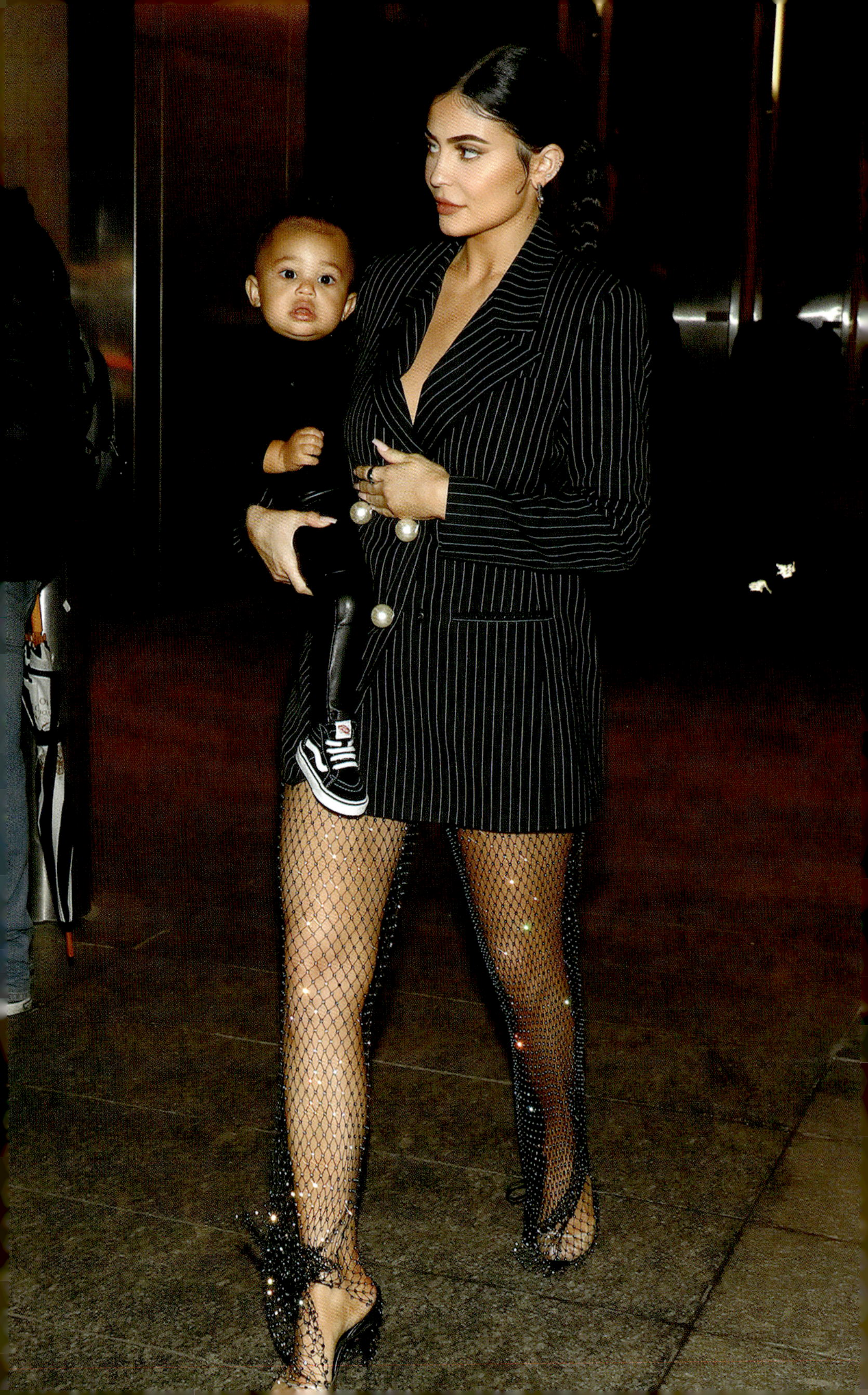

> **Kylie Jenner claims that Stormi loves listening to Scott's music.**

Scott was excited about being a new father. At the same time, he acknowledged that his career kept him out on the road much of the time. This made it difficult for Scott to be with Jenner and Stormi as much as he would have liked. The couple had adapted to their busy realities by spending "Stormi Saturdays" together. Jenner was willing to fly Stormi to wherever Scott was currently working or performing. Scott has joked that Stormi had more stamps in her passport before her first birthday than most people collect in their lifetimes.

Some of Stormi's travels have been to visit the Webster family in Texas. Scott brought Jenner and Stormi to Houston via private jet when Stormi was just nine weeks old. Scott's immediate family had met her earlier in Los Angeles, but Scott was excited to share his daughter with

STORMI IN THE SPOTLIGHT

Kylie Jenner was only nine years old when her family began filming their reality television show. She has spent most of her life in the spotlight. That same spotlight now shines on Scott and Stormi as well. Stormi often appears on Jenner's Instagram and Snapchat. Yet Jenner has expressed that she wants Stormi to make her own decisions about how public or private to make her life. When she's old enough, it will be her choice whether or not to be on reality television.

69

> In 2019, Jenner bought a billboard in Los Angeles, California, as a birthday present for Scott.

members of his extended family. He threw a party for the occasion complete with many expensive storm-themed floral arrangements. A few weeks later, Jenner threw her own big event by renting out the entire Six Flags amusement park for Scott, Jenner, and all their friends. It was in honor of Scott's twenty-sixth birthday. Guests left with custom hoodies. Jenner even had a cake made in the shape of a roller coaster with her, Scott, and Stormi riding along.

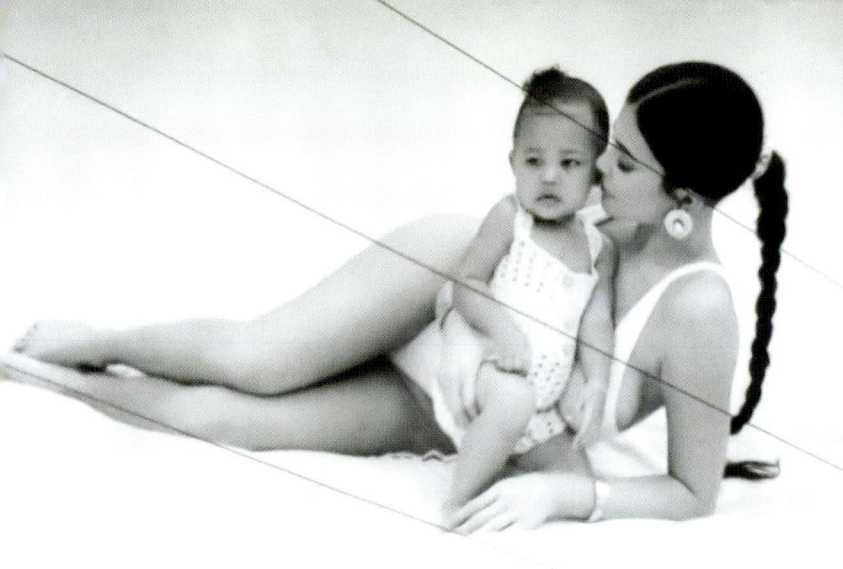

PARENTHOOD AND COUPLEHOOD

Though Jenner and Scott have made it clear that Stormi is their number one priority, they still made plenty

Jenner and Scott discussed their family and their time in the spotlight in their *GQ* interview.

> "But when you first have a baby in your arms, it's uncontrollable, it just takes over your whole body. I never thought I could just love something so hard, it's crazy."[7]
> – Travis Scott

of time for each other. They posted on social media about visiting Turks and Caicos as well as relaxing in France. They also attended the 2018 Met Gala together in coordinated outfits.

In July 2018, Scott and Jenner appeared on the cover of *GQ*, which was their first magazine cover together. In the cover story, Scott and Jenner opened up about their relationship in ways they hadn't before, even on social media. They spoke about learning to ignore the nasty rumors people often aim at the Kardashian/Jenner family. Both also acknowledged how difficult it was for the two of them to be apart so frequently.

The two agreed to keep their relationship private and focus on their life together out of the spotlight. Luckily, Jenner had the means to hop on a plane and join Scott wherever he was. They understood that being parents means working through trying moments to stay solid as Stormi's mom and dad.

GQ

TRAVIS + KYLIE

TO BE CONTINUED

There is no question Scott's relationship with Jenner has boosted his career. Scott was known for being a relatively shy rapper before the two started dating. After they began dating, Scott graced gossip magazines and celebrity fan pages. He also began to open up more in interviews. Though Scott was clear that he was not dating Jenner to advance his career, his music nonetheless benefited from her Snapchat stories and Instagram posts. Fellow rapper Nicki Minaj even called out the couple for using Jenner's social media to promote Scott's music. Minaj argued that the Scott/Jenner relationship had a direct impact on Scott's album sales, saying on Twitter, "Travis sold over 50K of these [VIP packages Jenner publicized] with no

KEEPING UP WITH SCOTT AND JENNER

The Scott/Jenner relationship had another interesting crossover into the music world. Scott's mentor and longtime collaborator, Kanye West, is married to Kim Kardashian West. She is Jenner's older half-sister. Kardashian West is also the reality television star who first brought the Kardashian name to pop culture's center stage more than a decade ago. Scott has long referred to Kanye West as family. If he and Jenner had been married, Scott and West would have become just that. Stormi is a cousin of West's four children, North, Saint, Chicago, and Psalm.

requirement of redeeming the album! . . . He knows he doesn't have the #1 album this week."[8]

Scott and Jenner had become one of music and social media's most important power couples. As a couple with such extreme celebrity, rumors of marriage, secret engagement, or even that their relationship was going up in smoke had surrounded them. However, in early fall 2019, speculations were confirmed that the two had drifted apart and were no longer together. Some thought they might get back together in the future. For now, the two said, they would both plan on being involved in parenting Stormi.

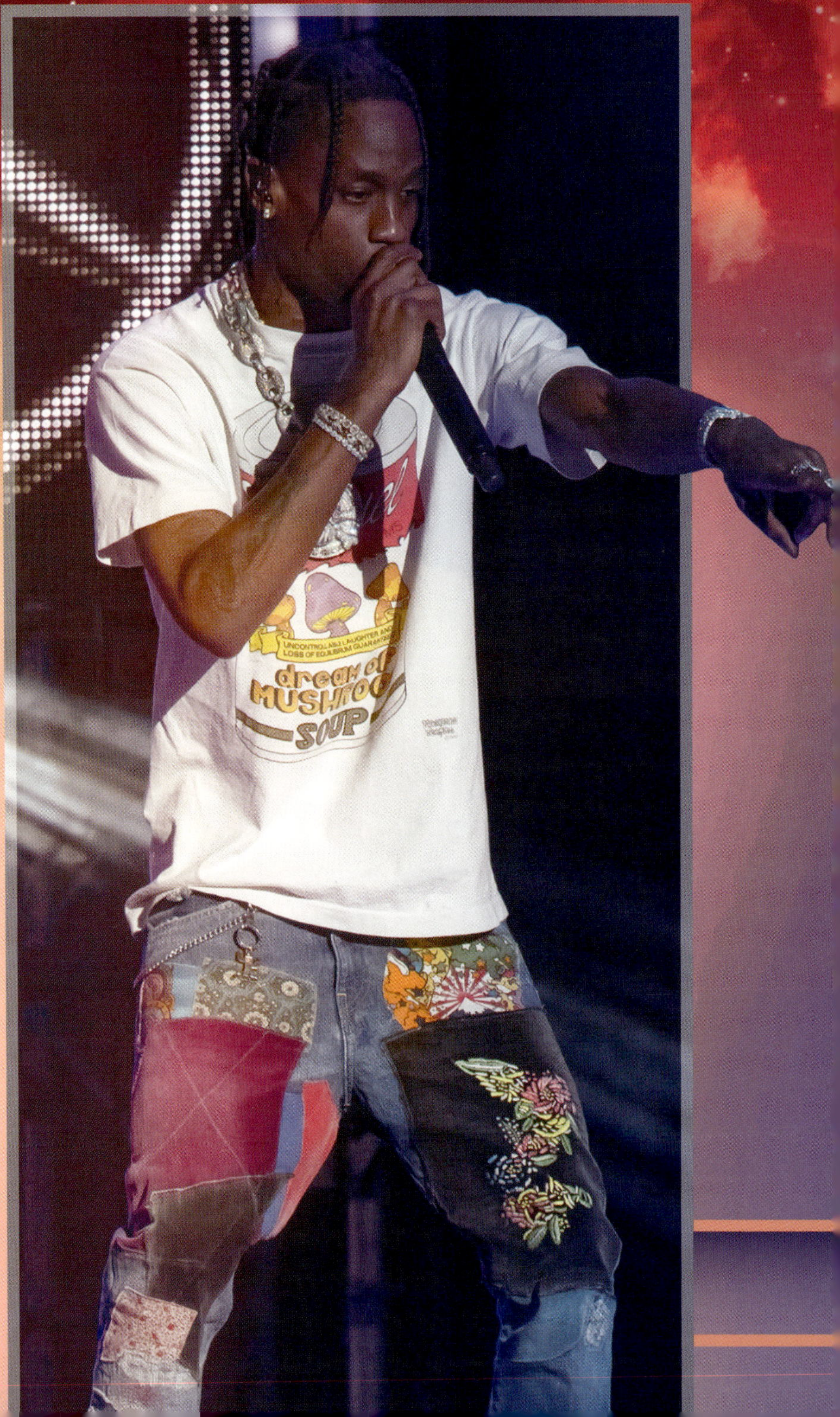
dream of
SOUP

ASTROWORLD

Chapter SEVEN

After a year of touring and working on other projects, Scott was ready to release new music. He formed a rap duo called Huncho Jack with the rapper Quavo. They hinted at an album for months, repeatedly pushing back the release date. Finally, *Huncho Jack, Jack Huncho* was released on December 21, 2017.

Critics were lukewarm on Quavo and Scott's debut album and did not think it was a standout. Quavo and Scott had worked together for years. Both were known for their larger-than-life personalities. Critics had hoped that their collaboration would yield a blockbuster. That proved not to be the case. *Pitchfork* wrote that the album "feels lethargic," adding, "*Huncho Jack*'s liveliness tends to come from everywhere except Quavo and Travis Scott."[1] Nonetheless, the album still debuted at Number 3 on the *Billboard* 200 and Number 1 on *Billboard*'s Top R&B/Hip-Hop and Top Rap Albums.

Luckily for Scott, his next biggest success was just around the corner. He was about to release his most

---

Scott performed songs from *Astroworld* on various TV shows to promote the album.

successful album yet, *Astroworld*. As with previous Scott projects, the album was both promised and delayed for months. Scott originally announced the title in May 2016 when he also announced *Birds in the Trap Sing McKnight*. At that time, he hinted on Twitter at a 2017 release for the album. At the time, he had no idea that he was soon to fall in love and conceive a baby, which undoubtedly distracted him—even if just a little—from album production.

Scott felt a connection to the AstroWorld theme park, which was torn down in 2005.

BUILDING EXCITEMENT

Scott shared on Twitter that he chose the name *Astroworld* from a Houston amusement park that was torn down in 2005 in order to make space for apartment buildings. The metaphor for the album was clear: Scott was going to return the joy and exhilaration Houston had taken away from him as a child. He was going to give it back in the form of music.

> "They tore down AstroWorld to build more apartment space. That's what it's going to sound like, like taking an amusement park away from kids. We want it back. We want the building back. That's why I'm doing it. It took the fun out of the city."[2]
> – *Travis Scott*

From the outset, *Astroworld* was intended to be the natural next step after the music released in *Rodeo*. *Birds in the Trap Sing McKnight*, conversely, was only an interlude. With *Astroworld*, Scott finally felt like he was back home.

Scott released the album's first single, "Butterfly Effect," in May 2017, just prior to when he and Jenner got their matching butterfly tattoos. "Butterfly Effect" quickly went platinum. It peaked at Number 50 on the *Billboard* Top 100. Fans and critics expected *Astroworld* to be released in the first quarter of 2018, but that date came and passed as well.

In July 2018, Scott headed to Hawaii with a team of artists and producers. News outlets reported that they would be finishing *Astroworld* at last. On July 27 and later July 30, giant, inflatable golden replicas of Scott's head appeared around the United States. One of the heads appeared above Amoeba Records in Los Angeles. The retailer is a Hollywood landmark that markets itself as the world's largest independent record store. A second inflatable head popped up in Times Square in New York City.

A third made an appearance outside Houston at Minute Maid Park, home of baseball's Houston Astros. Scott then announced on Twitter that *Astroworld* would be out later that week. He released a video trailer with an

THE ORIGINAL ASTROWORLD

AstroWorld was a 104-acre (42 ha) theme park in the Houston area that operated from 1968 through 2005. At its peak, the park featured some 45 rides, including multiple roller coasters. The company that owned the park at the time of its closure was Six Flags, which owns and operates amusement parks around the United States. Many of the coasters at AstroWorld were moved to other Six Flags parks after AstroWorld closed. Scott has talked about some of the attractions at AstroWorld that he remembers from his youth. They include a 20-story free-fall tower called Dungeon Drop and a loop roller coaster called Greezed Lightnin'. Greezed Lightnin' moved both forward and backward.

Scott used inflatable balloons shaped like his head to help promote his tour and album.

excerpt of the song "Stargazing." The album dropped on August 3, 2018.

The *Astroworld* single "Sicko Mode" was Scott's most successful track yet, going quintuple platinum by February 2019. "Sicko Mode" peaked at Number 1 on the *Billboard* Top 100. It also became the first hip-hop song in the chart's 60-year history to spend more than 30 weeks in the top ten. The song, which featured additional vocals by Drake and Swae Lee, was nothing like a typical Number 1 single. It did not have a chorus or hook, and it featured three completely different beats that shifted abruptly from one to the next. It utilized many elements of "lo-fi"

Swae Lee is part of the hip-hop group Rae Sremmurd.

production. This means that some elements of the song intentionally sounded low quality in order to produce a different vibe. Scott uses these lo-fi sounds in many of his songs. "Sicko Mode" became a hit, proving again that Scott's music was truly unique.

HIP-HOP HIT

Two of *Astroworld*'s other singles, "Yosemite" and "Wake Up," also did well on the charts. But the album's success did not surprise Scott. In an interview with *GQ* before the album's release, Scott said *Astroworld* was the best music he'd ever made. Scott celebrated the album's success by buying himself a custom Eliantte chain and pendant worth $450,000.

As with other Scott projects, the album featured a who's who of hip-hop talent. Guest performers included Drake, Swae Lee, Frank Ocean, Quavo, The Weeknd, and Kid Cudi, among others. Even music legend Stevie Wonder made an appearance.

Astroworld became Scott's first album to go double-platinum, selling and streaming more than two million units. *Rolling Stone* named it the sixth-best album of 2018. British music magazine *NME* called *Astroworld* "a lush, complex, and extraordinarily accomplished album."[3] One *Rolling Stone* writer had a more muted review, arguing that the second half of the album left something to be desired. However, he also said that *Astroworld* was the "first time that [Scott's] music has actually matched [his] aspirations."[4] *Pitchfork* called it "a sticky, humid, psychedelic world with dazzling production and odd pleasures at every turn."[5]

WISH YOU WERE HERE

Astroworld's dazzle did not end with the album. Scott began traveling with shows on the Astroworld—Wish

You Were Here Tour. The first leg of the tour spanned dates from November to December 2018. The second leg featured Scott crisscrossing the United States from January until March 2019. This time, Scott traded the giant robotic bird for an inflatable astronaut. The same golden inflatable Scott head showed up once again. Onstage, there were also rideable roller coasters, an inverted Ferris wheel, fireworks, and pyrotechnics. Lucky fans were pulled onstage to climb aboard the rides while Scott jammed in the background. One show even featured Jenner. She documented her ride on the roller coaster on her phone while Scott rapped along to "Antidote." Artists Sheck Wes, Gunna, and Trippie Redd opened for Scott during the tour. Other artists, including Kendrick Lamar and Drake, made the occasional appearance to rap along on "Goosebumps" and "Sicko Mode."

    As has become customary, the Astroworld—Wish You Were Here tour offered fans plenty of Travis Scott merchandise. Scott proved his business savvy once again with a new merchandising strategy. Every 24 hours for nine days, new products appeared on Scott's website. This rapid turnover encouraged fans to check in each day. They had to act quickly if they wanted to own one of the many limited-edition items before they sold out.

Most important, each of the products, no matter the size or the price, came with a digital copy of *Astroworld*. As a result, each product sale racked up an equivalent album sale. This helped *Astroworld*'s total numbers skyrocket. There is no way to know if fans who bought merchandise would have purchased the album anyway as opposed to simply listening to it on a streaming service. Regardless, *GQ* called the new rollout strategy "ingenius."[6] Since the rise of streaming services, artists often depend on selling products to make up for album revenue they would have captured without streaming. In this unique setup, Scott found a way to do both.

A NOD TO STORMI

Astroworld was Scott's first album after meeting Jenner and becoming a father. It was no surprise that its contents reflected some of these changes. Multiple tracks referenced

HELPING GET OUT THE VOTE

In October 2018, Scott took a break from preparing for the Astroworld—Wish You Were Here Tour to encourage fellow Texans to vote in the 2018 midterm elections. He appeared at a rally in his hometown of Houston. He encouraged young voters to make their voices heard at the polls. The rally featured Beto O'Rourke, a Democratic candidate who was running for a US Senate seat held by Republican Ted Cruz.

COVER ART

Scott's albums are artistic musical creations. In addition, each album cover reflects the talents of renowned visual artists. *Astroworld* featured the work of artist and videographer David LaChapelle, who has worked with famous musicians including Elton John, Mariah Carey, and Whitney Houston. The artwork for *Huncho Jack, Jack Huncho* was done by Ralph Steadman, who was 81 at the time of the album's release. Steadman is known for working closely with famed journalist and writer Hunter S. Thompson on the artwork for the cult classic novel *Fear and Loathing in Las Vegas*. For *Birds in the Trap Sing McKnight*, Scott enlisted British fashion photographer Nick Knight. That same year Knight had photographed the Queen of England and Prince Charles for the Queen's 90th birthday.

Jenner and her success, as well as Stormi. Stormi had become one of pop culture's most famous 2018 babies. Not only was "Coffee Bean" written about Scott's relationship with Jenner, but references to Jenner can be heard on "Stargazing," "Skeletons," and "Wake Up." On "Sicko Mode," Scott raps, "Pass this to my daughter, I'ma show her what it took / Baby mama cover *Forbes*, got these other b****** shook, yeah."[7]

Astroworld even served as an inspiration for Stormi's first birthday party, appropriately titled StormiWorld. Jenner's Instagram account documented the extravagant party for all of her followers to see. Guests entered the party through a giant inflatable Stormi head. It was similar to the golden Scott head that had become synonymous with his *Astroworld* album. Her party also included carnival rides, a room full of bubbles, costumed princesses, and a room full of teddy bears. There were even costumed sharks performing her favorite song, "Baby Shark." Scott and Jenner had truly created a baby friendly version of AstroWorld, the amusement park that had shut down back in 2005.

Scott's concerts often feature pyrotechnic and light displays.

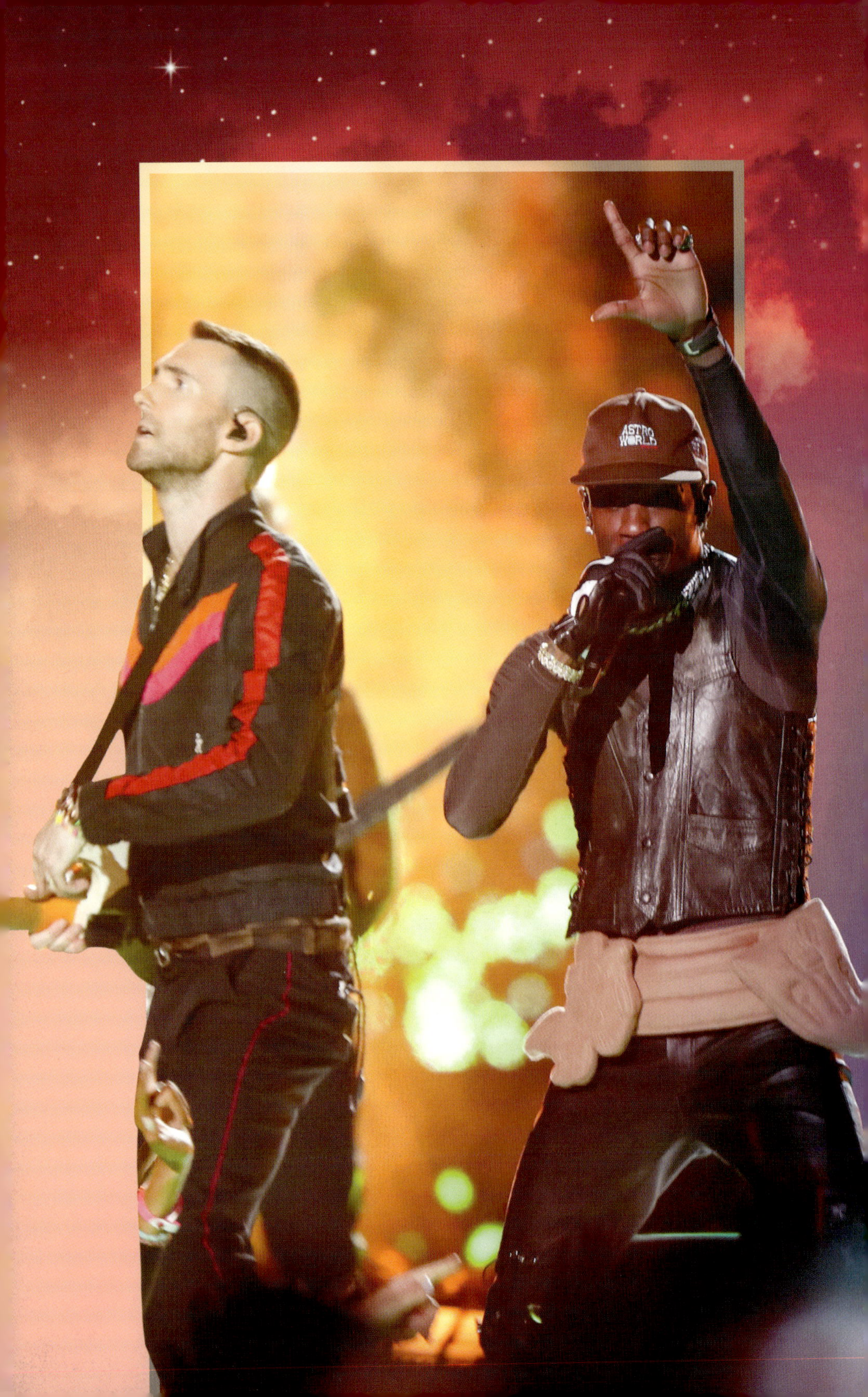
ASTRO
WORLD

THE SKY'S THE LIMIT

Chapter EIGHT

In October 2018, Scott made his debut as a musical guest on *Saturday Night Live*. He was accompanied by host Awkwafina, a rapper and actress. He performed a medley of "Skeletons" and "Astrothunder." It was the first time he'd performed "Astrothunder" live. He did it on a stage designed to resemble an amusement park. More surprising, though, were the musicians who accompanied him. Scott enlisted the help of John Mayer, Tame Impala's Kevin Parker, and producer and longtime Scott collaborator Mike Dean. In addition to the traditional music performances, Scott appeared in one of the show's sketches.

Just four short months later, Scott had a second nationally broadcast performance. He performed "Sicko Mode" at the Super Bowl LIII Halftime Show in front of the entire stadium as well as millions of viewers at home.

Scott performed at Super Bowl LIII along with Adam Levine, *left*, from the band Maroon 5.

Awkwafina hosted *Saturday Night Live* when Scott appeared on the show.

In exchange for the performance, Scott insisted that the National Football League join him in making a $500,000 joint donation to Dream Corps.[1] Dream Corps is an organization that tackles racial disparities and injustices by lifting up people of color in relation to environmental justice, criminal justice reform, and opportunities in the tech sector. Several artists had refused to perform at the Super Bowl due to controversy around the treatment of players who chose to kneel during the national anthem. Scott didn't want to pass up the opportunity to bring his music to millions, but he wanted his performance to make an impact on communities like the one he'd grown up in.

> "My whole story is straight mythical. It's tangible, but it's also what life could be."[2]
>
> – Travis Scott

One week later, Scott performed on television again. The string of performances made it clear that Scott's hard work and talent had made him very famous. Scott had been nominated for multiple awards at the 2019 Grammy Awards, held in February in Los Angeles. While he had been featured on other Grammy-winning tracks before, including SZA's "Love Galore" and Kanye West's "New Slaves," this was the first time he was nominated for his own song. *Astroworld* was nominated for Best Rap Album, and "Sicko Mode" was nominated for both Best Rap Performance and Best Rap Song.

Though he didn't win any Grammys, the nominations secured Scott's spot in hip-hop history. His performance at the awards show moved from a slow rendition of "Stop Trying to Be God" to the high-energy rap of "No Bystanders." He rapped from inside a cage on the stage, and nearly 100 people stormed the cage and climbed the bars. Scott ended the set by diving into the mosh pit around him.

EXPANDING INTO FASHION

In addition to setting trends in music, Scott has become a fashion icon. He has helped design collections with British label Maharishi, Austrian designer Helmut Lang, and the Australian-based company Ksubi. Scott says his interest in fashion goes back to his childhood. His mother bought him a Helmut Lang shirt when he was in high school. As a kid, he kept a blog and posted pictures of collections and pieces he liked. His favorites included items from brands such as Margiela, Louis Vuitton, Billionaire Boys Club, and Chanel.

Scott has appeared in campaigns for Nike, Fenty by Puma, Bape, Alexander Wang, Saint Laurent, and others. After attending a Paris Fashion Week runway show, he rocked a piece

HIP-HOP FASHION

Hip-hop music and fashion have been connected since the genre's rise in the 1980s. Hip-hop fashion always has been linked to what it means to be young and African American in America. In the 1980s, hoodies and sagging pants might have been used to hide cans of spray paint, express solidarity with prisoners, or simply rebel against society. These days, it's much more common to find rappers wearing high-end designers such as Givenchy or Louis Vuitton. According to Sacha Jenkins, who directed the documentary Fresh Dressed about hip-hop fashion, "It's like being a conquerer [sic] – you're buying into the notion of superiority."[3]

from the highly anticipated Supreme x Louis Vuitton collection. He even walked the runway during New York Fashion Week in 2015 for Mark McNairy's show.

In September 2018, Scott turned his fashion sense into a community service project. A student from Houston's Eisenhower High School reached out to Scott on Twitter. The student asked whether it would be okay to use the *Astroworld* cover art for her class's senior T-shirt. Scott replied, asking whether it would be okay if he just designed the shirts himself. Two months later, the students opened boxes of custom tees. They featured the words "wish you were here" alongside the school's name in a rainbow font, complete with a smiling globe. On the back, squeezed in between a giant "2019," were the words "enjoy the ride." There is

HOUSTON MUSIC SCENE

While East Coast and West Coast hip-hop were long dominant, many other areas of the United States produce their own unique sounds. Hip-hop is as integral to local culture as any other artistic medium. Houston has led the way for southern rap, with years of hip-hop history under its belt. The Houston-based group Geto Boys is credited as one of the first groups to give southern rap its name. The Houston-based label Rap-A-Lot Records is the longest-running independent imprint in the genre. While Scott and Beyoncé may be the most famous artists from Houston, rappers such as DJ Screw, Z-Ro, Bun-B, and Slim Thug all carry the Houston sound.

also a line that appears to be Scott's handwriting. It says, "Sincerely, Travis Scott."[4]

GIVING BACK TO HOUSTON

While Scott's career has taken him around the country, his heart never strays far from Houston. In early 2019, Scott donated $100,000 to Workshop Houston.[5] The group serves Houston youth with after school and summer classes related to dance, theater, fashion, graphic

During his performance at the Astroworld Festival, Scott strapped in to a circular roller coaster and looped upside down.

design, academic enrichment, and music production—specifically, making beats, just as Scott used to do in his bedroom as a teenager. He also funded a special event to honor and celebrate his hometown. He called it the Astroworld Festival.

The festival featured a carousel, a Ferris wheel, carnival swings, circus performers, and an amazing lineup of musicians including Lil Wayne, Rae Sremmurd, Post Malone, and Young Thug. There also were newcomers including Gunna, Smokepurpp, Trippie Redd, and Sheck Wes, as well as a number of veteran Houston rappers. Some 40,000 people attended the festival.[6]

On February 13, 2019, Scott was playing a show in Houston when two surprise guests appeared onstage. Right before ending his set with "Sicko Mode," Scott turned around to see Houston mayor Sylvester Turner and his daughter Ashley. The two presented Scott with a key to the city of Houston. Mayor Turner cited Scott's successful past year and major contributions to Houston as the reasons behind such an honor, and he told the audience that Houston owed much to Scott for what he'd done for the city. The mayor also promised to bring a new amusement park back to the city to help replace Scott's beloved AstroWorld.

NEW SPOTLIGHTS

Scott has proven himself to be a groundbreaking artist, pushing at creative boundaries in performance, production, merchandising, and more. In an interview on the talk show *Ellen*, Scott indicated his next project might be yet another genre-bender, implying that his next project might be a weeklong play designed around music. In addition, Scott has indicated that his next steps might include a return to school. In December 2018, Scott turned professor for a day and taught a class on his creative process at Harvard University. The class was a hit, and it led him to consider applying to the school himself.

Whether shouting an Auto-Tuned "It's lit!" on a track, chasing down music

THE CHANGING FACE OF MUSIC

In 2017, the Nielsen Music research firm released a surprising statistic: hip-hop and R&B had taken over from rock as the most consumed genre of music in the United States. According to Nielsen's report, hip-hop and R&B accounted for a full quarter of all music consumed. Music industry analysts credit streaming for the rapid growth in the two genres. Increasingly, streaming brings fan favorites to the forefront. Listeners stream music that they like more often and, in turn, make it more popular. With hip-hop such a strong force in streaming, all indications are that it will only continue to grow in popularity.

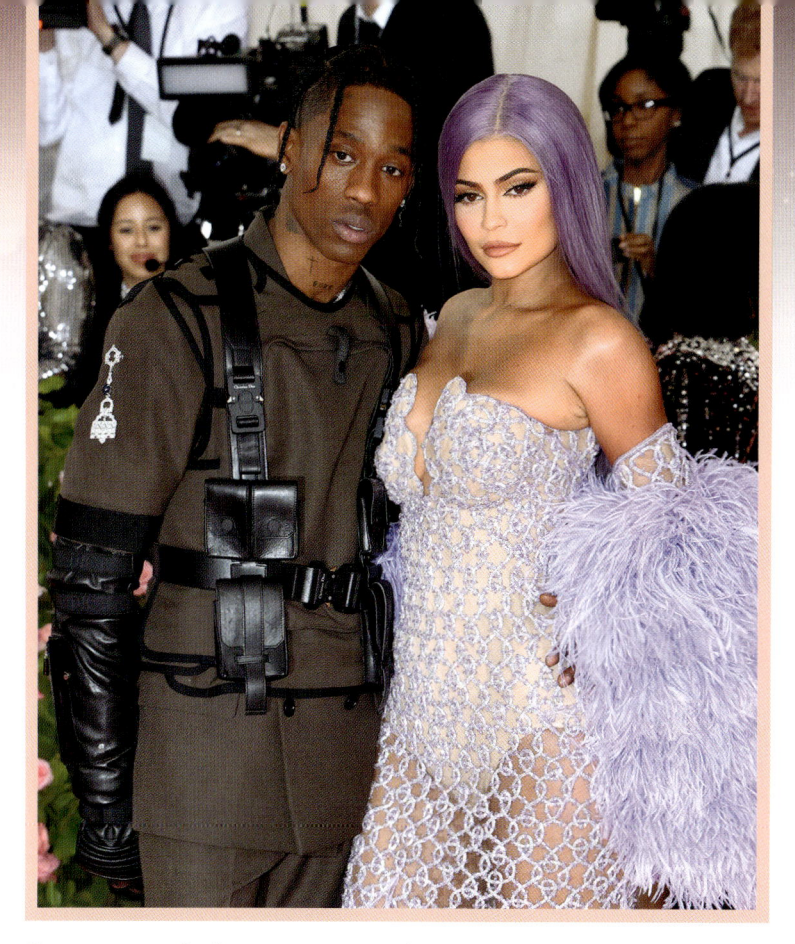

Scott attended many events in 2019, including the Met Gala.

industry executives, pushing boundaries onstage, or marveling at his baby daughter, Scott continues to amaze and entertain. What he ventures into next remains to be seen. There's little doubt the world already has been transformed by his persistence and commitment to his creative process. Scott's ability to work through every obstacle continues to inspire others who chase seemingly impossible dreams.

TIMELINE

1991
Travis Scott (Jacques Bermon Webster II) is born in Houston, Texas, on April 30.

2008
Scott graduates from Elkins High School in Missouri City, Texas.

2009
Scott and a friend release an EP as the Graduates but part ways after the release.

2012
Scott is credited on three tracks on G.O.O.D. Music's *Cruel Summer*.

2013
In May, Scott releases his first mixtape, *Owl Pharaoh*, to critical acclaim.

2014
In August, Scott releases the mixtape *Days before Rodeo*.

2015
In March, Scott and Young Thug kick off the Rodeo tour, setting a new standard in concert experiences.

Scott's debut solo album, *Rodeo*, hits the market in September.

2016

Scott's sophomore album, *Birds in the Trap Sing McKnight*, is released in September.

2017

In March, Scott announces the formation of his own record label, Cactus Jack Records.

In April, Scott meets Kylie Jenner at Coachella Valley Music and Arts Festival.

In December, Scott's album *Huncho Jack, Jack Huncho* is released.

2018

Stormi Webster, Scott's daughter with Kylie Jenner, is born in February.

In August, Scott releases his album *Astroworld*, which goes triple platinum.

In October, Scott performs on *Saturday Night Live*.

In November, Scott kicks off the Wish You Were Here Tour and ties merchandise sales to album sales.

2019

Scott performs live at Super Bowl LIII and the Grammy Awards in February.

Scott and Jenner drift apart in early fall.

ESSENTIAL FACTS

FULL NAME
Jacques Bermon Webster II

DATE OF BIRTH
April 30, 1991

PLACE OF BIRTH
Houston, Texas

PARENTS
Jacques Webster I and Wanda Webster

EDUCATION
Elkins High School, University of Texas at San Antonio

CAREER HIGHLIGHTS
Scott began creating music and publishing it on the online audio platform SoundCloud before graduating from high school. After forming two hip-hop duos in high school and college, Scott dropped out of school to travel back and forth between Los Angeles and New York to network with people in the music industry. Scott's talent came to the attention of rapper T.I., who signed him to his record label as an artist. Scott also got connected to Kanye West and began to work as a producer for Kanye's G.O.O.D. Music label. Since then, Scott has released two mixtapes and three studio albums, has been nominated for multiple Grammy awards, and has seen his work top both the *Billboard* 200 album listing and the *Billboard* Hot 100 for singles. He has been nominated for several Grammys, performed at the Super Bowl LIII Halftime Show, appeared on *Saturday Night Live*, and has uplifted and collaborated with visual artists and fashion designers alike.

ALBUMS

Owl Pharaoh (2013), *Days before Rodeo* (2014), *Rodeo* (2015), *Birds in the Trap Sing McKnight* (2016), *Huncho Jack, Jack Huncho* (2017), *Astroworld* (2018)

CONTRIBUTION TO HIP-HOP

Scott's raw talent and solid work ethic quickly translated into a successful artistic career. He distinguished himself through an innovative high-tech and diverse sound, and a willingness to collaborate and learn from the best in the industry. Scott is commended for his talent with music production and well-known for his ability to bring countless artists in on tracks he's created. He has consistently been at the forefront of a changing face of hip-hop, experimenting with increased Auto-Tune usage, dramatic beat shifts, and emotional lyrics.

CONFLICTS

For many years, Scott's lofty aspirations clashed with his parents' dreams for him, creating frequent family conflicts. Publicly, however, Scott's greatest controversies come from his hip-hop shows, where concertgoers have been seriously injured.

QUOTE

"I'm just here for good times, man. I want people to have the best time ever. Especially if they're around me. I feel like God put me here to help out with people's soul, man."

– Travis Scott

GLOSSARY

AUTO-TUNE
Software that allows sound engineers to digitally alter the pitch of sounds.

BEAT
The instrumental track of a hip-hop song, typically a pattern created by drums and other repetitive noises.

EXTENDED PLAY (EP)
A musical recording of several songs, longer than a single but shorter than an album.

HOOK
A catchy part of a song (but not necessarily the chorus) that draws in a listener.

MIXTAPE
A compilation of unreleased tracks, freestyle rap music, and DJ mixes of songs.

MOSH
A dance known for its violent nature; it includes jumping up and down and intentionally colliding with other audience members.

PAPARAZZI
Freelance photographers who take and sell photos of celebrities.

PLATINUM
An award, given by the Recording Industry Association of America (RIAA), that represents huge sales—500,000 albums for gold, 1 million for platinum, and 2 million or more for multiplatinum.

R&B
Rhythm and blues; a type of pop music of African American origin that has a soulful vocal style that features improvisation.

SYNTHESIZER
A machine that uses amplifiers and filters to create sound electronically.

ADDITIONAL RESOURCES

SELECTED BIBLIOGRAPHY

Green, Mark Anthony. "Kylie Jenner and Travis Scott on Love, Making It Work, and the Kardashian Curse." *GQ*, 17 Jul. 2018, gq.com. Accessed 17 Apr. 2019.

Guerra, Joey. "Travis Scott Gets Key to the City, Promise of a New Amusement Park at Astroworld Concert." *Houston Chronicle*, 14 Feb. 2019, houstonchronicle.com. Accessed 17 Apr. 2019.

Weiner, Jonah. "Travis Scott: In Orbit with Rap's Newest Superstar." *Rolling Stone*, 20 Dec. 2018, rollingstone.com. Accessed 17 Apr. 2019.

FURTHER READINGS

Burling, Alexis. *Drake: Hip-Hop Superstar*. Abdo, 2018.

Erickson, Angela. *So You Want to . . . Join the Music Industry: Here's the Info You Need*. Atlantic Publishing Group, 2017.

Lusted, Marcia Amidon. *Hip-Hop Music*. Abdo, 2018.

ONLINE RESOURCES

Booklinks
NONFICTION NETWORK
FREE! ONLINE NONFICTION RESOURCES

To learn more about Travis Scott, please visit abdobooklinks.com or scan this QR code. These links are routinely monitored and updated to provide the most current information available.

MORE INFORMATION

For more information on this subject, please contact or visit the following organizations:

BILLBOARD: CHARTS
billboard.com/charts

Billboard magazine, a magazine about the music industry, posts weekly charts showcasing the top music around the world. The *Billboard* Hot 100 showcases the 100 songs of the week that had the most plays, downloads, and purchases.

CITY OF HOUSTON MAYOR'S OFFICE OF CULTURAL AFFAIRS
901 Bagby Street
Houston, Texas 77002
houstontx.gov/culturalaffairs

The Mayor's Office of Cultural Affairs (MOCA) creates arts policies, groups, and projects in the city of Houston, Texas. It works with both visitors to the city as well as residents.

RECORDING ACADEMY
3030 Olympic Blvd.
Santa Monica, California 90404
grammy.com

The Recording Academy is an organization for musicians, songwriters, producers, and others who work in the music industry. It hosts and decides the winners of Grammy Awards and also runs MusiCares, which provides funding and other support to music artists in need.

SOURCE NOTES

CHAPTER 1. HIP-HOP TRANSFORMED
1. Insanul Ahmed. "Who Is Travi$ Scott?" *Complex*, 3 Oct. 2012, complex.com. Accessed 16 July 2019.
2. Simon Reynolds. "How Auto-Tune Revolutionized the Sound of Popular Music." *Pitchfork*, 17 Sept. 2018, pitchfork.com. Accessed 16 July 2019.
3. Thomas Gorton. "Travis Scott on *Astroworld*, Beauty, and His Fans." *Dazed Digital*, 28 Jan. 2019, dazeddigital.com. Accessed 16 July 2019.
4. Jonah Weiner. "Travis Scott: In Orbit with Rap's Newest Superstar." *Rolling Stone*, 20 Dec. 2018, rollingstone.com. Accessed 16 July 2019.
5. Gary Trust. "Travis Scott Scores First *Billboard* Hot 100 Leader." *Billboard*, 3 Dec. 2018, billboard.com. Accessed 16 July 2019.

CHAPTER 2. GROWING UP IN H-TOWN
1. Insanul Ahmed. "Who Is Travi$ Scott?" *Complex*, 3 Oct. 2012, complex.com. Accessed 16 July 2019.
2. Ahmed, "Who Is Travi$ Scott?"

CHAPTER 3. ALL OR NOTHING
1. James Petulla. "What Does a Music Producer Do?" *Recording Connection*, 2019, recordingconnection.com. Accessed 16 July 2019.
2. Insanul Ahmed. "Who Is Travi$ Scott?" *Complex*, 3 Oct. 2012, complex.com. Accessed 16 July 2019.
3. "Sin City." *Genius Lyrics*, n.d., genius.com. Accessed 16 July 2019.

CHAPTER 4. *OWL PHARAOH* AND *DAYS BEFORE RODEO*
1. Ralph Bristout. "Travi$ Scott—'Owl Pharaoh' Mixtape Review." *XXL Mag*, 23 May 2013, xxlmag.com. Accessed 16 July 2019.
2. Insanul Ahmed. "Who Is Travi$ Scott?" *Complex*, 3 Oct. 2012, complex.com. Accessed 16 July 2019.
3. Bristout, "Travi$ Scott."
4. Frazier Tharpe. "I Tried Not to Die at Travi$ Scott and Young Thug's Show Last Night." *Complex*, 13 Mar. 2015, complex.com. Accessed 16 July 2019.
5. Lia McGarrigle. "Travis Scott Drops 'Free the Rage' Mugshot Tee, but You've Only Got 48 Hours to Cop." *Highsnobiety*, 19 May 2017, highsnobiety.com. Accessed 16 July 2019.

CHAPTER 5. *RODEO* AND *BIRDS IN THE TRAP SING MCKNIGHT*

1. Jeff Ihaza. "Travi$ Scott Was Thrilled to Work with Justin Bieber on 'Maria I'm Drunk.'" *Fader*, 10 Sept. 2015, thefader.com. Accessed 16 July 2019.
2. "Travis Scott Action Figure Multi." *Stock X*, n.d., stockx.com. Accessed 16 July 2019.
3. "Anti: Deluxe Edition." *Rihanna Now*, n.d., rihannanow.com. Accessed 16 July 2019.
4. Elias Leight. "Travis Scott Talks 'Straight to the Meat' Second Album." *Rolling Stone*, 2 Sept. 2016, rollingstone.com. Accessed 16 July 2019.
5. Camille Augustin. "Travi$ Scott Discusses 'Rodeo' Album, Producing and More with Clique TV." *Vibe*, 8 Oct. 2015, vibe.com. Accessed 16 July 2019.
6. "Travis Scott Steps Up as a Maestro on 'Birds in the Trap Sing McKnight.'" *XXL*, 9 Sept. 2016, xxlmag.com. Accessed 5 Aug. 2019.

CHAPTER 6. KYLIE AND STORMI

1. Kate Talbot. "5 Social Media Lessons to Learn from Kylie Jenner." *Forbes*, 24 July 2018, forbes.com. Accessed 22 July 2019.
2. Natalie Robehmed. "At 21, Kylie Jenner Becomes the Youngest Self-Made Billionaire Ever." *Forbes*, 5 Mar. 2019, forbes.com. Accessed 16 July 2019.
3. Jonah Weiner. "Travis Scott: In Orbit with Rap's Newest Superstar." *Rolling Stone*, 20 Dec. 2018, rollingstone.com. Accessed 16 July 2019.
4. @trvisXX. "2.1.18 4 ever New rager in town. !!!" *Twitter*, 4 Feb. 2018, 3:01 p.m., twitter.com. Accessed 16 July 2019.
5. Laura Beck. "Kylie Jenner and Travis Scott Emerge for First Time Since Becoming Parents." *Cosmopolitan*, 25 Feb. 2018, cosmopolitan.com. Accessed 16 July 2019.
6. Mark Anthony Green. "Kylie Jenner and Travis Scott on Love, Making It Work, and the Kardashian Curse." *GQ*, 17 July 2018, gq.com. Accessed 17 Apr. 2019.
7. Sarah Jacoby. "Travis Scott Says Watching Kylie Jenner Give Birth Was 'Really Scary.'" *Self*, 13 Nov. 2018, self.com. Accessed 16 July 2019.
8. Cam Wolf. "Travis Scott Used Merch to Beat Out Nicki Minaj on the Charts." *GQ*, 20 Aug. 2018, gq.com. Accessed 16 July 2019.

CONTINUED

SOURCE NOTES

CHAPTER 7. *ASTROWORLD*

1. Brian Josephs. "Travis Scott/Quavo: Huncho Jack, Jack Huncho." *Pitchfork*, 3 Jan. 2018, pitchfork.com. Accessed 16 July 2019.

2. Chris Mench. "Houston's Mayor Wants to Build a New Amusement Park Because of Travis Scott's 'Astroworld.'" *Genius*, 14 Feb. 2019, genius.com. Accessed 16 July 2019.

3. Jordan Bassett. "Travis Scott—'Astroworld' Review." *NME*, 3 Aug. 2018, nme.com. Accessed 16 July 2019.

4. Christopher R. Weingarten. "Review: Travis Scott Starts Living Up to His Ambitions on 'Astroworld.'" *Rolling Stone*, 7 Aug. 2018, rollingstone.com. Accessed 16 July 2019.

5. Larry Fitzmaurice. "Travis Scott: Astroworld." *Pitchfork*, 7 Aug. 2018, pitchfork.com. Accessed 16 July 2019.

6. Cam Wolf. "Travis Scott Used Merch to Beat Out Nicki Minaj on the Charts." *GQ*, 20 Aug. 2018, gq.com. Accessed 16 July 2019.

7. "Sicko Mode." *Genius*, n.d., genius.com. Accessed 16 July 2019.

CHAPTER 8. THE SKY'S THE LIMIT

1. Jem Aswad. "Travis Scott and NFL to Donate $500,000 to Non-Profit Ahead of Super Bowl Performance." *Variety*, 13 Jan. 2019, variety.com. Accessed 22 July 2019.

2. Lawrence Schlossman. "Idol Worship." *Complex*, December 2015, complex.com. Accessed 16 July 2019.

3. Lauren Cochrane. "So Fresh and So Clean: A Brief History of Fashion and Hip-Hop." *Guardian*, 27 Oct. 2015, theguardian.com. Accessed 22 July 2019.

4. Brooke Bobb. "Travis Scott Played Fashion Santa to Seniors at This Houston High School." *Vogue*, 18 Dec. 2018, vogue.com. Accessed 16 July 2019.

5. Andrew Dansby. "Houston Rapper Travis Scott Donates $100,000 to Workshop Houston." *Houston Chronicle*, 8 Jan. 2019, houstonchronicle.com. Accessed 22 July 2019.

6. "Astroworld: The Best of Travis Scott's 'Wish You Were Here' Tour in Houston." *ABC Eyewitness News 13*, 19 Nov. 2018, abc13.com. Accessed 22 July 2019.

INDEX

A$AP Ferg, 44
Astroworld, 11, 78, 79–83, 85–87, 91, 93
AstroWorld (theme park), 80, 87, 95
Astroworld Festival, 95
Auto-Tune, 8, 10, 44, 56, 96
Awkwafina, 89

Baker, Donny, 30
beats, 8, 10, 21, 22, 37, 39, 41, 58, 81, 95
BET Awards, 11
Beyoncé, 16–17, 93
Big Sean, 6, 40, 47
Billboard, 11, 18, 54, 58, 59, 66, 77, 79, 81
Birds in the Trap Sing McKnight, 57–59, 78, 79, 86
Bon Iver. *See* Vernon, Justin.

Cactus Jack Records, 59
Cher, 10
Classmates, the, 29–30
Coachella Valley Music and Arts Festival, 59–60, 63, 64
Complex, 49
Cruel Summer, 40–41, 43–44

Days before Rodeo, 46–47, 53
Dean, Mike, 57, 89
DeGeneres, Ellen, 11
Dr. Dre, 9
Drake, 11, 60, 81, 83, 84
Dream Corps, 90

Eisenhower High School, 93–94
Ellen, 96
Epic Records, 6, 39, 53
Eric, Jason, 29–30

Forbes, 63, 86
Future, 54

G.O.O.D. Music, 6, 30–31, 40–41
Geto Boys, 93
GQ, 50, 67, 72, 82, 85
Graduates, the, 29
Grammy Awards, 11, 91
Grand Hustle Records, 6, 8, 41, 44, 53

Harvard University, 96
Holloway, Chris, 29
Houston Astros, 80
Huncho Jack, 77
Huncho Jack, Jack Huncho, 77, 86

jazz, 9, 19, 21
Jenner, Kylie, 63–75, 79, 84, 85–86, 87

Kardashian West, Kim, 74
Keeping Up with the Kardashians, 63, 69
Kid Cudi, 6, 15, 18, 40, 58, 83
Ksubi, 92
Kylie Cosmetics, 63, 64

LaChapelle, David, 86
Lamar, Kendrick, 11, 21, 58, 84
Lang, Helmut, 92
Lil Wayne, 95
Lollapalooza, 51
Los Angeles, California, 5, 6, 32, 34–35, 41, 69, 80, 91

Mayer, John, 89
Meek Mill, 44
merchandise, 51, 56, 84–85, 96
Met Gala, 64, 72
Migos, 46, 57
Minaj, Nicki, 74–75
mixtapes, 11, 30, 43, 44, 46, 47
moshing, 49, 50, 91
MTV Video Music Awards, 58

National Football League (NFL), 90
NBA 2K19, 57
New York, New York, 6, 30, 41, 80
NME, 83
Notorious B.I.G., 41

Ocean, Frank, 83
OG Chess. *See* Eric, Jason.
O'Rourke, Beto, 85
Owl Pharaoh, 11, 43, 44, 46

Parker, Kevin, 89
Pitchfork, 77, 83
Post Malone, 35, 95
Pusha T, 6, 40

Quavo, 58, 77, 83

Rae Sremmurd, 95
Rap-A-Lot Records, 93
Rihanna, 11, 56–57
Rodeo, 47, 53–54, 56, 58, 79
Rolling Stone, 54, 59, 66, 83

Saturday Night Live, 89
Shakur, Tupac, 41
Six Flags, 70, 80

social media, 47, 63, 64, 67, 69, 72, 74, 75, 78, 79, 80, 93
SoundCloud, 35, 43, 46
SPIN, 46
Sugarhill Gang, 21
Super Bowl, 11, 89–91
Swae Lee, 81, 83
synthesizers, 9
SZA, 91

T.I., 5, 6, 8, 11, 35, 37, 44, 46–47, 53, 54
Thompson, Hunter S., 86
Times Square, 80
tours, 17, 47–51, 59–60, 63, 64, 77, 83–85
Turner, Sylvester, 95
21 Savage, 58
2 Chainz, 40, 46, 54

University of Texas at San Antonio, 24, 27, 34

Vernon, Justin, 44
Very Good Beats, 41
Vuitton, Louis, 92

Waxx, Mike, 30–31, 37
Webster, Stormi, 66–72, 74, 85–87
West, Kanye, 6, 11, 30–31, 37–40, 41, 44, 47, 48, 54, 74, 91, 93
Workshop Houston, 94

XXL Mag, 46, 54, 59

Young Thug, 46–49, 54, 58, 95

111

ABOUT THE AUTHOR

Jill Wheeler is the author of more than 300 nonfiction titles for young readers. Her interests include biographies, along with natural and behavioral sciences. She lives in Minneapolis, Minnesota, where she enjoys sailing, riding motorcycles, and reading.

JUL 2020

UNION COUNTY PUBLIC LIBRARY
316 E. Windsor St., Monroe, NC 28112